CONTENTS

		PAGE
I.	INTRODUCTION	9
II.	SUBJECTS	17
III.	TEMPERAMENTS	92
IV.	METHODS	149
V.	APPENDIX	177

I

INTRODUCTION

LET me say at once that I regard the works of
Mr. Henry James as those most worthy of
attention by the critics—most worthy of
attention of all the work that is to-day pouring
from the groaning presses of continents. In
saying this I conceal for the moment my private
opinion—which doesn't in the least matter to
anyone, though it is an opinion that can hardly
be called anything but mature—that Mr.
James is the greatest of living writers and in
consequence, for me, the greatest of living men.

I might, that is to say, have thought, as I
have, that Mr. James is the greatest of living
men without ever contemplating thus setting
out to write a book about him. A man may
be supremely great and offer no opportunity
for comment of any kind. I cannot, that is to
say, imagine any serious writer setting to work
to say anything about Shakespeare, about
Turgenieff, or for the matter of that about
Nelson or Moltke. There are people who just
" are," consummate in various degrees, perfect

engines of providence. It is a little difficult, or at any rate it would call for a great number of words to explain exactly what I mean; but in order to avoid the danger of being considered paradoxical I will venture here and now upon a rough digest of that number of words so as to plan out the ground of this book.

Thus, when I say that no one can write much about Shakespeare or Turgenieff I say it because, thank God, we know nothing whatever about Shakespeare. He is personally nothing but a wise smile and a couple of anecdotes. And his work, considered from a literary point of view, is too consummate for any literary comment. You can annotate his words and his historic matter to an extent that has provided us with fifty libraries of pedagogic dullness or of anecdotal interest, as the case may be; but the beautiful spirit of the man you cannot in any way touch. So in a sense it is with Turgenieff whom Mr. James calls at one moment " my distinguished " friend," at another " the amiable Russian "; but finally, being worthy of himself, he styles him " the beautiful genius."

And that is all that can be said about Turgenieff—he was " the beautiful genius." Again, thank God, we know as little of his personality as we know of Shakespeare's. I do not mean to say that he is as tangibly indefinite a solar myth; we know enough about him to be able to say that he was not the late Mr. Pobiedonostieff, procurator of the Holy Synod, and to be certain that his work was not written by the late Count Tolstoy. Fragments of his personality are, in fact, recoverable here and there. These two eyes have seen him in a studio; a rather nasty Slav, Russian, or Pole has written a rather nasty book about him. In this he attempts to place " the beautiful genius " in an unfavourable light as sneering at his great French fellow-workers. To-day Young Russia sneers at *him* for not being a Collectivist, a Nihilist, a Marxist, a Syndicalist or what you will. And Young England, which is always sycophantically at the bidding of any whining Intellectual, whether Celt or Slav, repeats the lament of Young Russia that Turgenieff was not a Collectivist, a Marxist, and all the rest of it. And against Turgenieff Young England erects the banner of Dostoievsky, as if the fame of that portentous writer of enormous detective stories, that sad man with the native Slav genius for telling immensely long and formless tales, must destroy the art, the poetry and the exquisiteness that are in the works of " the beautiful genius." . . .

At any rate, precious little is recoverable of the personality of Turgenieff. We know that he shot partridges which perhaps he shouldn't have done. We know also that he purchased cakes of scented soap for a mistress whom perhaps he shouldn't—or perhaps he should—have had. But the fact is that he lived partly amongst men of letters who could not find anything much to say about his work and partly amongst gentlefolk who did not want to say much about his personality. Therefore he remains, baffling and enticing, but practically, too, only a smile and a couple of anecdotes. About his work the critic can say no more than he can about that of Shakespeare. Its surface is too compact, is too polished; the critical pickaxe or geological hammer just cannot get up a little chunk of *that* marble for chemical analysis. It exists as the grass exists which the good God made to grow, and that is the end of the matter.

Similarly, as I have said, with Nelson and Field-Marshal von Moltke. These were " the beautiful geniuses " of embattled nations. Their genius probably consisted in their being ready to take chances. You may analyse the strategy of Nelson just as you may analyse that of Von Moltke, but you cannot say why God was on their side, and until you can say that you cannot very well say much that is to the point. Nelson ought never to have fought the battle of Trafalgar; the chances, in that particular spot of the Bay of Biscay, were seven to one that such an unfavourable wind must there spring up as should frustrate the manœuvres ordered from the *Victory*. Similarly, Moltke should never have fought Gravelotte; the chances were twenty-seven to one that the Crown Prince of Saxony would not arrive in time; the chances were eleven to one in favour of the French rifle; there was practically no chance that the German troops would face that hill of death in the final charge and, in the event of any of these evil chances taking effect, final disaster was all that Germany could have expected.

Thus, once more there is very little to be said about these matters.

There is very little in short to be said about pure genius. It is just a thing that is. And there is nothing left for us, who are in the end but the stuff with which to fill graveyards, to say more than that marvellous are the ways of Providence that gives to a few so much and to the vast many nothing at all. But there remains a second—by no means secondary —order of great people into whose work it is possible, and very profitable, minutely to enquire. For, if you can't say much about Moltke you can discover pretty easily, and descant for long upon, the strategy of Marlborough ; if you can't say much about Shakespeare you might write several books about the craftsmanship of Goethe ; if Johannes Sebastian Bach defies the pen as far as his peculiar magic is concerned, the pen can find endless objects for its activity in the music drama of Richard Wagner ; or, if you can't find out how Turgenieff did any single blessed thing you could write a volume about the wording of one paragraph by Flaubert. To this latter category belong the works of Mr. Henry James.

Mr. Henry James has of course his share of the talent which can't be defined. He has, that is to say, plenty of personality. You could no more confound him, say, with Théophile Gautier than you could confound Homer with Dante or with Quintus Horatius Flaccus, but in addition to having—to *being*—a temperament Mr. James has a conscious craftsmanship. His temperament we may define clearly enough if Providence provides the words, though we couldn't, any of us, say where in the world he got it from. But his craftsmanship, his conscious literary modifications, his changes of word for word, the

INTRODUCTION

maturing of his muse, the way in which quite
consciously he mellows his vintages, all these
things he has very efficiently betrayed to us.
And it is this betrayal that makes one select
his work rather than those of Monsieur Anatole
France, of Monsieur Henri de Regnier ; for the
matter of that of Monsieur André Gide, of
Mr. Joseph Conrad, or Mr. W. H. Hudson—to
name the other really great writers of our day
—for analysis. With any one of these five fine
spirits you might go a long way. You might
define their geniuses, you might dimly guess
at their methods, but you can't—as you can
with Mr. James—say quite definitely that here
he changed the words " she answered " into
the words " she indefinitely responded." Mr.
James has in fact given hostages to all of us
who will be at the pains of a little grubbing up
these definite facts as to his methods ; the
others have given us practically nothing of the
sort, so that, in their cases, if one submitted
them to the pains of vivisection one must leave
the whole question of their methods very much
to conjecture. In planning out therefore the
following book I propose firstly to state
why this writer appears to me to be the
greatest author of our day—which is as much
as to say why he is valuable to the world ;
secondly, I shall attempt to define his tem-

perament to the extent of trying to show how far it is a mirror of the concrete things and the invisible tendencies of our day ; and in the third place I shall attempt for the instruction of this day of ours, to define, as clearly as may be, what are the methods of this distinguished writer. This I am aware is, as the American poet said, " all sorts of a job."

I am aware too that the charges may be brought against me that, firstly, in these pages I have made a profuse use of the "I". I can't help that. I have wanted to be plain and, in matters difficult to express, such locutions as " the present writer " add confusion. These are the present writer's personal impressions of our author's work put as clearly as the medium will allow.

Moreover, there are in these pages a great many disquisitions on the " conditions " of modern life. But for these also I do not apologise. You cannot write about a great writer of Actualities without giving some account of the times in which he lived. You cannot write about Euripides and ignore Athens. (I am aware that it is usual to do so !)

II

SUBJECTS

I HAVE said that I consider the author of *The Spoils of Poynton* the greatest writer now living; let me now bring forward the reasons for this belief. Greatness as it appears to me is a quality possibly connected with, but certainly not solely dependent upon, artistry. I should hesitate in fact to say that Mr. James is the greatest artist now living; indeed, I should hesitate to say whether any one artist was ever greater than any other artist. This, however, is a point upon which I by no means wish to dogmatise. If I say that I regard Christina Rossetti as as great an artist as, let us say, Horace, or that I regard Beckford who wrote the letters from Portugal as as great an artist as Prosper Mérimée or Shakespeare or Mr. W. H. Hudson or François Villon, I mean simply that artistry appears to me to be just a quality that either you have or you haven't. If you have it you are

17

as great but no greater than any other artist, and every other artist is as great but no greater than yourself. I do not mean to say that the effects of your art upon the world may not be greater or less than that of any other artist. It is very likely that the actual effect of Christina Rossetti upon the present age is greater than that of the writer of the single line :

ἠράμεν μὲν ἐγό σέθεν, ᾿Αθι, παλαῖ ποτὰ

yet it would be absurd to deny that Sappho was as great an artist as the author of Goblin Market, just as it would be absurd to deny that the sculptor of the Winged Victory was as great an artist as Monsieur Rodin or Michael Angelo. It appears to me, then, that the quality of being an artist is such another quality as are beauty, race, honesty or fineness of temperament—a quality conferred by the gods upon the men whom they love.

But then again we come upon the use to which the artist will put the measure of the light vouchsafed him. God forbid that I should say that all artists are equal in their output, their moral values or, for the matter of that, in their technical industry. The works of Shakespeare are longer than the Bible ; François Villon was a scamp, whereas

SUBJECTS

Mr. James in a literary sense would adorn the society of any Cathedral close. Balzac poured out an unceasing stream of imaginings without any particular attention to methods. Flaubert was thinking of methods all day long.

I have said somewhere else that the supreme quality of art is to be interesting, and after some years of reflection upon the matter I do not get any further than that, though I can put it in another way. The real essence of art is a sense of appropriateness, almost as it were a sense of decency. The real artist feels for his subject a quality of chastity; whilst he is handling it he will no more introduce into it extraneous or unsuitable matter than a lady of niceness will go to the opera in the costume she reserves for the golf course. At the same time, this sense of appropriateness in the texture and conception of the work will no more affect, say, the takings of a railway company than will the opera costume of any lady however negligent or however strong-minded. Yet undoubtedly writers may quite remarkably affect the takings of railway companies which, in an Anglo-Saxon community, may well be taken to be the most important things in the world. If we put it upon a very small scale it is, I believe, statistically true that

19

one book brings in an income of £70,000 a year to the Great Western Railway Company, that book being Lorna Doone; for it is estimated that, every year, 60,000 people visit Exmoor and the neighbourhood on account of the glamour that Mr. Blackmore threw over that quite charming country. Or think, again, of all the shipping, the railway, the transport and the motor companies that are kept alive by pilgrims to the shrine of one writer or another at Stratford-on-Avon. Or consider, again, how whole populations have been set moving by writings about various regions. How much population has the vast city which we inhabit gained from the poetic imagining that the streets of London are paved with gold; or what do the plains of Canada, the mountains of Central North America or the islands in the Gulf of Mexico not owe to the imaginings of poets of one kind or another? Consider how the Dominion of Canada resented the poetic appellation of Our Lady of the Snows—and why? Simply because Canada was afraid that intending emigrants might be frightened away by that epithet, shadowing as it seemed to do an arctic climate.

That such greatness then may appertain to the usually despised profession of writing few will probably deny. Nay, the great railway companies themselves give evidence of this fact, for, if you will write to any one of them and state that it is your intention to write a book about any given tract of country served by their line, they will at once present you free of charge with a first-class season ticket over the whole of their system. But they will never stop to enquire whether you are an artist or not, or whether you possess a sense of appropriateness or of the chastity of your subject.

It is not however this type of greatness that I claim to any great extent for the author of *The American Scene*. For, roughly speaking, when the reader embarks upon that magnificent book of impressions he reads for many pages with a sense of deep, of complete, and finally of utter, non-comprehension. And bewilderment accompanies him through the long process of perusal. But when you close the book—at that very moment a sense of extraordinary reality overwhelms you. You will find that you have actually been in New York whose note is the scream of trolley wheels upon inefficiently laid granite setts ; you will find that you have actually been at Manhattan Beach, where ladies, so lacking in elusiveness, say and do the odd, queer things in the high, queer voices. It is, *The American Scene*, an

amazing piece of artistry, but I do not imagine
that it ever made any single soul desire to
join the scant company of rubber-necks who
visit the United States. Let us not however
deny to this distinguished author all claims
to this particular form of greatness, for many
of us have undoubtedly done no more in
visiting the country of the Lilies than follow
in the footsteps of the author of *A Little
Tour in France*.

Or, again, how many New Englanders may
not have been brought to the Old World by
the limpid, beautiful and delightful phrases
of what we now call the early James? What
may not *Daisy Miller, The Four Meetings,
A Passionate Pilgrim, Roderick Hudson*, or,
for the matter of that, *The Spoils of Poynton*,
have done to swell the receipts, in the 80's
and the 90's, of the American touring agencies?
But it is not distinctively in this light that we
have to view the greatness of our eminent
Subject. It is not especially as the conductor
of populations across mountains and floods
that the figure of Mr. James *saute,* as you
might say, *aux yeux*. His greatness, to put it
succinctly, is that of the historian—the
historian of one, of two, and possibly of three
or more, civilisations. (Let it be understood
that in this section I am in no way considering

Mr. James' art, but merely his services to the Republic.) And, roughly, speaking the two services that a writer can render to the State are, firstly, that he can induce its inhabitants to become more moral; secondly, he can render them better educated. Mr. James is practically no sort of moralist at all. I do not mean to say that any word he has ever written need bring the blush to the cheek of any inhabitant of any Cathedral close whose society, as I have said, Mr. James' literary figure would so eminently adorn. But Mr. James' conscious purpose in writing can obviously never have been to make people better. It might be possible that a perusal of *What Maisie Knew* might show to several erring personages that the Divorce Courts are exceedingly troublesome places to get into; or, to read *The Spoils of Poynton*, might shock various other persons, engaged in family quarrels about money, into frames of mind less sordid. It is conceivable, in fact, that the works of Mr. James may have been a civilising agency. But I can observe little if any trace in all the voluminous works of this writer of a desire to leave humanity any better than he found it. He observes the characters of his work with a comic or with a patronising spirit;

whether they be the victims or the oppressors we seem to hear him saying of them: " Poor dears." He would speak of " poor dear Maisie " just as he would speak of " poor dear Mrs. Gereth " who lost the Spoils; or just as, for the matter of that, you may hear him speak of " poor dear Flaubert," " poor dear Shakespeare " or " poor dear Balzac," Napoleon the First, Napoleon the Third, or anybody in the world. Compassion or any trace of a desire to be helpful are in fact almost entirely wanting in the works of this impersonal writer. They are absent in a way that characterises no other author known to me. Flaubert, heaven knows, is impersonal enough; yet it is impossible to read Madame Bovary and to mark Emma's frantic running from pillar to post to pick up a little money, whilst the net is closing all round her, without feeling that Flaubert had an immense sense of pity, and that Flaubert, had he come across Emma in real life, would have lent her considerable sums of money. Similarly with Mr. James' great master, it is impossible to read Lisa or Smoke or A Sportsman's Sketches, impersonal observation although they all may be, without feeling Turgenieff's immense sympathy with the mental or material sufferings of his characters. The absence of this charac-

teristic is extraordinarily striking in Mr. James'
work. Maisie is for him just a child in a
basement. Or, if you will read either the
original or the revised version of *The Four
Meetings* you will be almost appalled by this
peculiar passionlessness. *The Four Meetings*
is the story of a New England schoolmistress
with a passionate yearning to see Europe.
She gets as far as Havre upon one occasion
and is promptly sponged upon by a worthless
relation who extracts from her all her money,
so that she has to return to New England on
the very evening of her arrival. And, some
time afterwards, when she is again beginning
to save up a little money for the purpose of
visiting Europe—and it is impossible to say
how intensely and how horribly Mr. James
has rendered her yearning to see Chamounix
or Venice—she is descended upon by the
soi-disant wife of the worthless cousin, the
runaway wife of someone like a small French
hairdresser. This lady, giving herself out to
be a Countess, battens upon the New England
schoolmistress until the very day of the
latter lady's death. In whichever version
we read this *nouvelle* we are compelled to say
that it is unsurpassed in the literature of
any language or of any age. It is the perfect
" longish short story." First published in

1883 and, presumably, written at about that date, this story has been considerably re-written for Volume XVI of Mr. James' complete edition which was published in 1909. These facts are merely bibliographical, but what jumps at your eyes in reading either version is the singular pitilessness of the narrator. The story, that is to say, is put into the mouth of a third party who writes in the first person. In the first version this narrator seems to present himself as a quiet, gentle, observant young New Englander. In the latter version, he appears to be a sardonic, rather florid, rather garrulous, international American in the later years of his life.[1] But in neither case, whether as a young and modest man or an elderly and patronising personality, does the narrator give any evidence of its even occurring to him that he might conceivably render some assistance to the poor victim of her infamous connections. It never apparently occurs to either narrator to offer to lend the lady at Havre, after she had been robbed, five or six pounds so that she might at least spend a day or two in Paris after having come so far. And it never seems to have occurred to either narrator to say to the poor New England school marm

[1] See Appendix.

that the cuckoo in her particular nest was no Countess at all, but merely an infamous adventuress who should be instantly turned out of the little weather-boarded house. No, the narrator just lets the thing go on and concludes with the scoffing remark : " I could feel how right my poor friend had been in her conviction that she should still see something of that dear old Europe." This statement, implying as it did that a fragment of Europe, in the shape of the sham Countess, had descended upon that poor New England victim, seems to me to be one of the most pitiless sentences ever penned by the hand of man.

I am aware that these remarks are open to the objection that, if the narrator had made the offer of the five or six pounds, and, if it had been accepted, the story would have gone to pieces. But of course the New England schoolmistress would never have accepted the money just as she would never have believed any vague surmises that the narrator might have made as to the Countess' origin. The real fact is that Mr. James knows very well that he was giving just an extra turn to the tragedy of the story by making his narrator so abnormally unhelpful. And the other fact remains: obviously Mr. James does not consider that he came into this world to make it any better otherwise than it could be bettered by his observation and the setting down of his observations. He does not, that is to say, expect to improve the world by advocating anything. He doesn't suggest that divorce laws or marriage laws or prison laws or social laws should be altered. He merely gives you material. Upon the views which you may gather from this material you are at liberty to form your verdict and to direct your votes when the questions of divorce, marriage, crime, or society may come before you in a practical sense.

That, then, is the secret of Mr. James' greatness in so far as it applies to the outer world. As to what may be his personal aims, as to what may go on within the cavernous recesses of his artist's mind, we have simply no means of knowing, and very likely he has simply no means of knowing himself. Nay, I will even go so far as to say that he couldn't by any possibility be the great writer that he is if he had any public aims. *What Maisie Knew*, that is to say, would certainly not have been a passionless masterpiece if Mr. James had thought that it was his business, as a writer, passionately to uphold on the one hand the claim of marriage to be a sacrament, or on the other passionately to decry the claim of the marriage law to any existence whatever. Indeed, whatever the figure of Mr. James, the individual, may be, the figure of Mr. James, the writer, is that of a philosophic anarchist. In the whole array of Mr. James' books, except for the mention of the employment of a solicitor—and even that appears to be regarded as the vaguest of expedients—in *The Spoils of Poynton*, and except for the fact that the divorce laws obviously have some—but a quite shadily defined—influence upon the career of Maisie, I cannot recall any single instance of the mention of the law, or for the matter of that of a policeman in any one of Mr. James' quarter of a century of volumes of fiction. This is how that formidable engine, the Law of England, seems to present itself to this distinguished writer :—

The litigation had seemed interminable — so *What Maisie Knew* opens—and had, in fact, been complicated ; but by the decision on the Appeal the judgment of the Divorce Court was confirmed as to the assignment of the child. The father, who, though bespattered from head to foot, had made good his case, was, in pursuance of this triumph, appointed to keep her : it was not so much that the mother's character had been more absolutely damaged as that the brilliancy of a lady's complexion (and this lady's in court was immensely remarked) might be more regarded as showing the spots.

This, then, with its charming vagueness, is apparently all the legal paraphernalia upon which this long book is founded. Yet it is characteristic that, in defiance of English legal procedure, a lady's complexion should have any effect or be remarked on at all in an Appeal Court. In a Divisional Court of the Probate, Divorce and Admiralty Division, Mrs. Farange's complexion might have played its part in the eyes of the jury. But in the Appeal Court, consisting as it does of three judges and no jury; in which the witnesses are not re-examined and not necessarily present at all; which devotes the whole of its time to the consideration of legal points—not one of which could by any possibility turn upon the quantity of peroxide used by a lady—the question of the state of her skin could not, I believe, have had any influence at all. In a similar way the tremendous engine of the law is disposed of in *The Spoils of Poynton. The Spoils of Poynton* turns upon whether a mother or a prospective daughter-in-law is to grab the beautiful contents of one of the most beautiful houses in England :—

"And did you think," [Fleda Vetch asks the unfortunate son of the mother and fiancé of the prospective daughter-in-law], "your mother would see you?"

" I wasn't sure, but I thought it right to try—to put it to her kindly, don't you see ? If she won't see me, she has herself to thank. The only other way would have been to set the lawyers at her."

" I am glad you didn't do that."

" I'm dashed if I want to," Owen honestly responded. " But what's a fellow to do if she won't meet a fellow ? "

" What do you call meeting a fellow ? " Fleda asked with a smile.

" Why, letting *me* tell her a dozen things she can have."

This was a transaction that Fleda had after a moment to give up trying to represent to herself. " If she won't do that—— ? " she went on.

" I'll leave it all to my solicitor. *He* won't let her off, by Jove. I know the fellow ! "

" That's horrible ! " said Fleda, looking at him in woe.

" It's utterly beastly."

And this, as regards the " plaintiff " in what might have been a protracted legal dispute, is to all intents and purposes all that is said about the law in this wonderful book. As regards the " defendant," the mother who for the moment is in possession of the "Spoils," who is sitting in the house and refusing to quit it, our author is a little more definite. But indeed Mrs. Gereth is a character of somewhat more definite will than are many that Mr.

James asks us to consider. And Mrs. Gereth, at least for a moment, looks at the situation quite definitely :—

> . . . Fleda asked Mrs. Gereth if she literally meant to shut herself up and stand a siege, or if it might be her idea to expose herself, more informally, to be dragged out of the house by constables.
> " Oh, I prefer the constables and the dragging ! " the heroine of Poynton had readily answered. " I want to make Owen and Mona do everything that will be most publicly odious." She gave it out as her one thought now to force them to a line that would dishonour them and dishonour the tradition they embodied. . . .

And, in the end, in spite of the threat of the solicitor and the other threat of submitting only to policemen, the question of the occupation of Poynton solves itself upon a purely moral note, as is to be expected in our author's works. In actual English life of to-day, given Mrs. Gereth with her tendencies which are those of the eternal brigand, and, given the Brigstocks, those perfectly English people—" the worst horror " of their house, called Waterbath, " was the acres of varnish, something advertised and smelly, with which everything was smeared : it was Fleda Vetch's conviction that the application of it by their own hands, and

hilariously shoving each other was the amuse-
ment of the Brigstocks on rainy days "—given
these exceedingly English people, with the
rather will-less but quite English figure of
Owen Gereth between them, the problem
would have become one, really, of affidavits,
of interim orders of the court, of the pur-
loining of small valuables, of false evidence
by servants, tradesmen, vicars' wives' companions and heaven knows whom. But ·for
Mr. James English life is a matter of smooth-
nesses, civilisations, and that very avoidance
of publicity which Mrs. Gereth felt to be her
strongest weapon.

The Brigstocks of Waterbath desired to
acquire Poynton by right of marriage :—

There had been in the first place the exquisite
old house itself, early Jacobean, supreme in every
part ; a provocation, an inspiration, the matchless
canvas for a picture. Then there had been her
[Mrs. Gereth's] husband's sympathy and generosity,
his knowledge and love, their perfect accord and
beautiful life together, twenty-six years of planning
and seeking, a long sunny harvest of taste and
curiosity. Lastly, she never denied, there had been
her personal gift, the genius, the passion, the patience
of the collector. . . .

" Don't you think it's rather jolly, the old shop ? "
Owen Gereth had asked his fiancée.

" Oh, it's all right," Mona Brigstock had graciously remarked ; and then they had, probably, with a slap on the back, run another race up or down a green bank.

And this the Brigstocks desired to acquire by marriage.

And the real ambition of the Brigstocks, their real passion, was as follows :—

At the end of five minutes the young lady from Waterbath suddenly and perversely said : " Why has she never had a winter garden thrown out ? If ever I have a place of my own I mean to have one."
Fleda, dismayed, could see the thing—something glazed and piped, on iron pillars, with untidy plants and cane sofas ; a shiny excrescence on the noble face of Poynton. She remembered at Waterbath a conservatory where she had caught a bad cold in the company of a stuffed cockatoo fastened to a tropical bough and a waterless fountain composed of shells stuck into some hardened paste. She asked Mona if her idea would be to make something like this conservatory ; to which Mona replied : " Oh, no, much finer ; we haven't got a winter garden at Waterbath."

Now nothing in the world could be a stronger passion than the passion of an English family, with their solicitors and the paraphernalia of the law at their back, to stick a small Crystal Palace on to the back of a Jacobean house like Poynton ; and nothing could be stronger than the determination of an English freebooter of the type of Mrs. Gereth to prevent their doing anything of the sort, to stick to Poynton, to mother Poynton, to go on adding in spite of straitened circumstances treasure to treasure. Mr. James has quite rightly discerned in this, his greatest book, that these passions are the very strongest that exist in English society of to-day. The Brigstocks would automatically call in a policeman ; Mrs. Gereth would desperately commandeer, steal, lie, swear false affidavits, allege undue influence, suborn false witnesses, and so on, these being the daily occupations of all quite good English families where questions of property are concerned.

But that hasn't been Mr. James' method in dealing with this subject. Being, as he so essentially is, an un-Americanised American, he couldn't in that way treat what he considered at the start and what, after many disillusionments, he would still like to consider—an ancient civilisation, the inhabitants of all these homes of ancient peace, the denizens of all these West End drawing-rooms and better class suburban garden parties. It isn't in fact Mr. James' business to treat of subjects that centre round Fleet Street, where are to be found amongst other monuments of our great civilisation, the Royal Courts of Justice. In the preface to one of his novels he has told us that he never could bring himself to treat of a " down town " subject—" down town " being the American expression for " business," since most of the business of New York is conducted between Fourteenth Street and the Battery, just as most of the business of London is conducted between the Law Courts and the eastern limit of the City proper. No, the spirit in which the negotiations attending The Spoils of Poynton is conducted is not in any way a " down town," but an " up town " spirit. In order to get away from the affidavits, the interim orders, and the writs, Mr. James introduces into his " affair " the figure of Fleda Vetch. And Fleda Vetch is, as you might say, the apotheosis of civilisation of the " up town " spirit—the spirit of that West End which is so distinctly not the spirit of the City, but which is so distinctly the spirit of whatever is creditable that our civilisation has to show. It is as if to a table of financiers, of " down town " or of city men, to a board of directors with their devious manners, their queer points of view, their obscure knowledges of wire-pulling, of bribery with shares, of rigging the market—as if, to such a body, a decent-minded individual from the West End or from a country house should have been introduced—as if, that is to say, Christ should come to Chicago or to any other " Third Floor Back." The chances would be that Our Lord would do little enough, but still He would have a chance. And this particular chance Mr. James chooses to give to his Fleda Vetch. She is an angel making a wonderful visit and, if the results do not end in the salvation of Poynton and if they do end in a great deal of pain of heart to Fleda herself, nevertheless the resultant of her visit is the preservation of the public decency. Her apparition practically puts into Mrs. Gereth's head the idea that Mona Brigstock may be outwitted and crushed by the attraction of Fleda far more effectually than by any buccaneering on her own part. And, in the presence of Fleda, Owen Gereth is struck with the idea that to serve writs upon his mother would be horrible, would be disgusting. Thus the story works itself out, down to the burning of Poynton, in an atmosphere of increasing delicacy. The case of " Gereth versus Gereth " and possibly of " Brigstock intervening " never got into the list ; it stopped, by the grace of Fleda, at the mention of the policemen and at the mention of the solicitor.

So that, roughly speaking, if Mr. James have any moral lesson to inculcate, that would be his formulation of his particular lesson—that a civilising personality introduced into an affair is better than any lawsuit. And it should be pointed out very carefully that nowhere does Mr. James in this story preach any change of the law. He appears to accept implicitly the state of things as it is. I don't mean to say that he doesn't, from the contemplation of the characters, crawling as it were around his serene footstool, discern the fact that some of them might like certain of our laws to be changed. Yet even this, in the mouths of his characters, amounts far more to a desire for a change in sentiment than for a change in legislation :—

[Mrs. Gereth] hated the effacement to which English usage reduced the widowed mother ; she had discoursed of it passionately to Fleda, and contrasted it with the beautiful homage paid by other countries to women in that position, women no better than herself, whom she had seen acclaimed and enthroned, whom she had known and envied ; she made, in short, as little as possible a secret of the injury, the bitterness she found in it. . . . Hadn't she often told Fleda of her friend Mme. de Jaume, the wittiest of women, but a small black crooked person, each of whose three boys when absent wrote to her every day of their lives. She had the house in Paris, she had the house in Poitou, she had more than in the lifetime of her husband—to whom, in spite of her appearance, she had afforded repeated calls for jealousy—because she was to have till the end of her days the supreme word about everything. It was easy to see how Mrs. Gereth would have given again and again her complexion, her figure, and even perhaps the spotless virtue she had still more successfully retained to have been the consecrated Mme. de Jaume. She wasn't, alas, and this was what she had at present a splendid occasion to protest against.

It is possible that in this last sentence we may discern the beginnings of a trace present in Mr. James' mind of the germs of what is now called militant suffragism. But it is none the less odd to observe that hitherto, as I have before said, what is principally in the mind of Mr. James' character is rather a change in sentiment than any change in the law. She desires more that a woman's son should write to her every day of her life—in which case she would be pretty sure to keep him off the Mona Brigstocks of the world—than any legislative enactment that a man should upon marriage make a compulsory settlement upon his wife, or upon his deathbed make in her favour compulsory testamentary bequests.

And the consideration, in memory of the whole range of Mr. James' work, doesn't seem to give me, in this respect, any other lesson.

I say " in memory " because, although ever since the age of eighteen I have read with attention every work of our distinguished author that I could at all lay my hands on, and although, for the purposes of this book, I have made a careful, textual comparison between the earlier stories of our author in their original form, and themselves decked out in the fine linen in which Mr. James' later years delight—all the same, I can't be said to have made any very German study of this author's works. After all, Germany with its annotators will long survive myself; more-over the French habit of writing immense and immensely trustworthy baccalaureate mono-graphs upon particular authors will also long outlive us and our day. Therefore I am presenting you rather with my impressions of our author's work than the outpourings of any note-books. This seems to me to be the proper method for dealing with an author who, more than anything else, is an impres-sionist. So that, when I say the only traces of the actions of the law to be found in

SUBJECTS

Mr. James' voluminous writings, I don't mean
to say that litigation is nowhere else mentioned in the quarter century of large volumes ;
I only mean to say that these passages in
What Maisie Knew and *The Spoils of Poynton*
are really the only ones that have made any
salient impression on my mind. I am, in
short, making for a definite purpose a carefully
studied exaggeration. Any fault-finder upon
the point of fact is at liberty to bring up
against me, for instance, that matchless *nouvelle* which is a part of the " late " James, and is
called *The Bench of Desolation.* I don't
know whether the actual bench in this particular case was the tribunal that tried the
action or whether it was the seat decorating
the parade upon which sat so frequently the
victim of his country's tricky laws. The story
—wonderful to relate—is the story of an action
for breach of promise. You can't of course
imagine any subject more preposterous for
Mr. James' treatment. And indeed he doesn't
treat it as far as the action is concerned,
though it comes, as near as Mr. James can
by any possibility be expected to come, to
the mention of writs, justifications, and the
rest of it. No indeed, this story of the ruin
and the subsequent salvation of a small
country tradesman gives you no more than,

as it were, the veriest echoes, heard in the suburbs—or at the seaside—of what is passing in Fleet Street where the Law Courts are. The small shopkeeper is sued for breach by a determined, masterful, and quite pleasant woman who is the last person that you would expect to take any such proceedings—who is in fact quite " civilised," quite the lady. The small shopkeeper—he deals in books and prints and is therefore himself of a comparatively scholarly and " civilised " kind—in his desperate efforts to pay off by instalments the heavy damages that were awarded against him, and also to provide for the slight extravagances of a rather silly little wife whom he eventually marries—sinks slowly down and down the hill of indigence. The wife dies ; bankruptcy confronts him ; then there turns up for his salvation the woman who has ruined him. She is wealthy ; she appears to own hotels— for you never can for the life of you tell quite definitely what any of Mr. James' characters own, any more than you ever know quite precisely what any of your own friends own. At any rate, she is quite blazingly wealthy. And she tells the ruined small shopkeeper that the whole of her intention in bringing the action for breach of promise was to provide for his old age. She had foreseen that the weak amiability of his so civilised character would eventually bring him to bankruptcy in any case. By getting out of him a largish sum which was partly capital and partly income, she has forced him to save, in, as it were, *her* money-box, the quite enviable sum which, by means of successful investment, management and re-investment she is thus, towards the end of his life, able to pour—with proper restrictions—into his lap.

Thus, it will appear that, although *The Bench of Desolation* is at first sight the story of a breach of promise case, it is in reality nothing of the sort. It concerns rather the device of a far-seeing woman to save a man from himself. I don't see that any particular moral is to be drawn from this story.

II

I don't, for the matter of that, see that any moral at all is to be drawn from any of Mr. James' work. For, if, upon the one hand, you get as far with *The Spoils of Poynton* or with *What Maisie Knew* as to say that one of their definite morals is that publicity and the odiousness of the Courts of Law are things to be avoided ; on the other hand, you might learn from *The Bench of Desolation* the simple lesson that the publicity and the odiousness of the Courts of Law may be turned to account by a clever woman to such an extent as to make, at any rate, something of a man out of a quite weak-kneed individual. In any case, the one moral for what it is worth may well counteract the other.

I made my first acquaintance with the works of our distinguished subject during my gentle youth which covered the last years of the 80's and the early 90's. I call it my "gentle youth" because, whatever may be the case with the youths of other people, my own early and late adolescence was a period for me of extreme submission to authority; it is only in fact in later life that I have become impatient of fools. The works of Mr. James, then, were thrust into my hands by the sort of brow-beating, "advanced" intellectuals who, let us say, founded the Fabian Society, the Independent Theatre Society, The Browning Society, or any of the numerous Societies that flourished or merely existed in the 90's. And, whilst these works were thrust into my hands, it was enjoined upon me to believe, I was in fact brow-beaten into trying to see—as if it were the ultimate end, the ultimate aim, the *causa causans* of our author's existence—in all Mr. James' books, from *Daisy Miller*—nay, from that very *Watch and Ward* which is now no more than a ghost in works of reference—to *The Spoils of Poynton* itself ; I was told to believe that, in *The Real Thing*, as in *The Lesson of the Master*, in the *Pension Beaurepas* as in *The Princess Casamassima*, the one thing for which I was to look was the Profound Moral Purpose.

Now the profound moral purpose of the 90's was a curious thing made up of socialism, free thought, the profession of free love going hand in hand with an intense sexual continence that to all intents and purposes ended in emasculation, and going along, also, hand in hand with lime-washed bedroom walls and other æsthetic paraphernalia. It was, that is to say, the profound moral purpose of the 90's, that really frightened me out of my life.

I never knew during the years when I was reading the early and the middle James, when I wasn't, in one way or the other, offending against the great moral purpose of the universe. And I used to read, say, *The Diary of a Man of Fifty* in the hope that there it would be plain—as it wasn't in any other terrestrial phenomena that had come under my view—that there, at least, that particular and very frightening

45

Figure in the Carpet, the moral purpose of the universe, would be made manifest. I read Mr. James, in fact, naively and gropingly, as the young read, in the hope of becoming a better Fabian and a wiser supporter of the Independent Theatre. But I could not square it out.

I could not square it out with the work of Mr. James any more than I could square it out with the world that we live in ; probably because the one is so like the other. I have said elsewhere that, considering that our contacts with humanity are nowadays so much a matter of acquaintanceship and so little a matter of friendship, considering that for ourselves, moving about as men do to-day, we may know so many men and so little of the lives of any one man, the greatest service that any novelist can render to the Republic, the greatest service that any one man can render to the State, is to draw an unbiassed picture of the world we live in. To beguile by pretty fancies, to lead armies, to invent new means of transport, to devise systems of irrigation—all these things are mere steps in the dark ; and it is very much to be doubted whether any lawgiver can, in the present state of things, be anything but a curse to society. It seems at least to be the property of almost every law that to-day we frame to be infinitely more of a flail to a large number of people than of a service to any living soul. Regarding the matter historically, we may safely say that the feudal system in its perfection has died out of the world except in the islands of Jersey, Guernsey, Alderney, and Sark. The middle ages with their empirical and tricky enactments against regrating and the like; the constitutional theories, such as they were, of the Commonwealth and the Stuart age, have disappeared; the Whiggism of Cobden and Bright, the bourgeois democracy of the first and third Republics and the oppressive, cruel, ignorant and blind theorising of later Fabianism have all died away. We stand to-day, in the matter of political theories, naked to the wind and blind to the sunlight. We have a sort of vague uneasy feeling that the old feudalism and the old union of Christendom beneath a spiritual headship may in the end be infinitely better than anything that was ever devised by the Mother of Parliaments in England, the Constituent Assemblies in France, or all the Rules of the Constitution of the United States. And, just at this moment when by the nature of things we know so many men and so little

47

of the lives of men, we are faced also by a sort of beggardom of political theories. It remains therefore for the novelist—and particularly for the realist among novelists—to give us the very matter upon which we shall build the theories of the new body politic. And, assuredly, the man who can do this for us, is conferring upon us a greater benefit than the man who can make two blades of grass grow where one grew before ; since what is the good of substituting two blades for one— what is the benefit to society at large if the only individual to benefit by it is some company promoter ?

That is the reason for my saying that I consider Mr. James to be the greatest man now living. He, more than anybody, has observed human society as it now is, and more than anybody has faithfully rendered his observations for us. It is perfectly true that his hunting grounds have been almost exclusively " up town " ones—that he has frequented the West End and the country house, practically never going once in his literary life east of Temple Bar or lower than Fourteenth Street. But a scientist has a perfect right—nay more, it is the absolute duty of the scientist—to limit his observations to the habits of lepidoptera, or to the bacilli of cancer

48

if he does not feel himself adapted for enquiry into the habits of bulls, bears, elephants or foxes. Mr. James, to put the matter shortly, has preferred to enquire into the habits of the comfortable classes and of their dependants, and no other human being has made the serious attempt to enquire with an unbiassed mind into the habits and necessities of any other class or race of the habitable globe as it is. That is why Mr. James deserves so well of the Republic.

I am aware that my penultimate statement is what is called a large proposition, but I think I am justified in making it. The English novel has hitherto occupied a very lowly position, whether in the world of art or in the world where sermons are preached, political speeches listened to, railway trains run, or ships plough the sea; and, in both these worlds, its lowly position has upon the whole been justified. The critic has been forced to say that the English novelist has hardly ever regarded his art as an art; the man of affairs has said that to read English novels was waste of time. And both the critic and man of affairs have hitherto been right. The worlds of art and affairs are widely different spheres, but that is not to say that they are spheres that should not interact one upon the other.

Indeed, my grand-aunt Eliza amply summed
the matter up, busy woman as she was, when
she exclaimed that sooner than be idle she
would take a book and read. But this attitude
is only justifiable in a world of affairs that
can't get hold of books worth reading. For,
when books are worth reading the world of
affairs that omits to read them is lost both
commercially and spiritually. You cannot
have a business community of any honesty
unless you have a literature to set a high
standard. And you could not even run a very
efficient cotton-spinning industry unless you
kept in your mind some idea of how fashions
change—some idea, that is to say, of the
psychology of dress of whatever class it is
that you have to cater for. The really efficient
maker of Manchester goods is the man whose
knowledge of psychology, the world over,
is so considerable that he will be able to say
considerably beforehand in what year cotton
frocks will be very largely worn in the West
End when it goes into the country, and in
what year woollen sweaters will take the
place of cotton frocks. Or, again, he should
be able to prophesy at what time an increased
demand for his wares will come from the East.
Now I do not mean to say that a study of the
works of Mr. Henry James, however close,

will show a manufacturer at precisely what moment *mousseline de laine* will supersede white cotton ; but a careful study of those same books would show that manufacturer what a tricky thing the psychology of the smart to smartish woman may be. It would give him, that is to say, tips as to the undesirability of keeping his eggs for too long all in the same basket. It might be said that the manufacturer might learn these things from the study of his own trade but, owing to some human fatality in the fabric trades, this is not the case. Do we not daily read that the English manufacturer—who is too busy to read novels—is being ousted all over the world by his German rival, a much more intelligent being and one whose reading of literature is so considerable as to be, by comparison, vast ? This is not paradox ; it is really a fact that the German manufacturing class do take an intense interest in literature.

I have recorded elsewhere my meeting, in a corridor train, a Jewish stocking merchant of Cologne who stated to me in accents of almost tearful sincerity that, if his daughter could marry a real but penniless poet he would willingly give her an enormous dower, whereas if she married a manufacturer he would give her only half the sum, and would insist upon the bridegroom making an at least equal settlement. This gentleman was then on his way to England where, owing to his subsequent exertions, his firm almost completely captured the woollen sweater-coat trade. The fact is that imagination is as useful a quality in a manufacturer as, let us say, attention to detail. And if my Jewish friend had kept himself as little in touch with the products of imagination as the English small tailors who were ruined by him—sweater-coats having, as the phrase is, almost entirely " knocked out tailor - mades "— my Jewish friend would have been as ruined as are the English tailors.

But, to return to the more tangible proposition that there are practically no English novels that are not artistically negligible, and that it would not be a waste of time, or at any rate that it would be any more than an agreeable occupation for leisure moments, to read. Let us for a moment survey the entire field.

I was once asked to write a history of the English novel—a technical history. I considered the idea at first with enthusiasm ; it appeared to be just exactly the job that I wanted. But, gradually, the glory of the

idea faded out as fade the hues of the dying
flying fish. As a matter of fact, there *is* no
technical history of the English novel. There
is, of course, a history. You could write about
the lives of Defoe and Fielding and Sarah
Fielding and Richardson and Scott and Dickens
and Thackeray and Meredith and all the rest
of them. But you can't find much more than
three sentences to say of the methods of any
one of them. They may have had great natures
or they may have been buoyant storytellers,
but of art they hadn't a pennyworth between
them, and they did not care even that amount
for analysis of human nature. I don't mean
to say that they weren't amusing or entertaining, or some of them romantic and others of
them calculated to take you out of yourself;
but, regarded as conscious literature their works
are just splendidly null. And regarded as in-
formers upon human nature they have hardly
the value of police reports which colour all the
characters black or white. They deal in
heroes and villains, those fabulous monsters;
which is as much as to say that they have
remained psychologically upon the level of
Sir John Mandeville. We attend upon their
performances as we attend the meetings at the
National Sports Club, and when the hero
bashes the villain one in the jaw we throw up

our caps and shout "hurray!" But that has nothing to do—nothing on earth to do, with the world we live in.

Mr. James has no connection with these amiable amateurs. If he is an un-Americanised American, as at the first glimpse we are tempted to call him, he is surely the least naturalised of all the English. And, indeed, it is only in our haste that we can speak of him as un-American. Actually he is the most American product that New England ever turned out. I don't mean to say that, arrayed in a top hat, with a shovelful of medals on his breast and decorated with a gaily-coloured scarf across his stomach, he goes hurrahing through the streets because some one, by buying up the Thirteenth Ward, has got in his nominee for district attorney. No, the " gettings in " of Mr. Henry James are of another order.

But let us go back to two gentlemen whom I have treated with scant courtesy—let us go back to Defoe and still more to Richardson, for, if we in the least wish to understand the figure of Mr. James we must consider the figure of the author of Clarissa. Defoe, in fact, was a realist of the city and of the mart. He touched boldly upon those " down town " subjects from which Mr. James' muse flees

with averted face. But Richardson was the
" up town," the West End realist of his day.
And it is amazing to consider how, tempera-
mentally, the author of Pamela foreshadows
for us the figure of the author of *The Golden
Bowl*. It is amazing, that is, until you come
to consider how it is obvious and predestined,

Mr. Henry James, the reader may reply,
comes to us from France, where he was the
pupil of Turgenieff. That is perfectly true.
But Richardson—the spirit of Richardson—
abandoning these isles to Fielding and the
Romanticists—crossed the Channel. It became re-incarnated in, it was the chief influence upon, Diderot and the Encyclopædists.
Diderot begot, as you might say, Chateaubriand and even Stendhal; and Stendhal
and Chateaubriand between them had for
children Flaubert, Maupassant, the Goncourts,
Gautier, and the very air of the very circle
in which Turgenieff and the young James went
about together. It is not my business to be
unnecessarily biographical, but I cannot resist
mentioning a glimpse of a letter that was
kindly afforded me by a French writer a little
time ago. The letter was written by Flaubert,
and recounts how Turgenieff had brought to
see him a young American who had enraged
Flaubert beyond belief. He had, this young

American, spoken disrespectfully of the style of Prosper Mérimée. Now, says in effect the great author of Madame Bovary, Prosper Mérimée was no great shakes. But that was more than he could stand from any American. . . .

That young American was Mr. James.

To come back, however, from this biographical digression—to which, however, I must later once more return—to come back to the question of what is the real greatness of Mr. James, I must allow myself an immensely long quotation from one of his prefaces—a quotation throwing light upon, or at least adumbrating the matter of why during all his literary life he remained so sedulously " up town."

What is more to the point is the moral I at present find myself drawing from the fact that, then turning over my American impressions, those proceeding from a brief but profusely peopled stay in New York, I should have fished up that none so very precious particle as one of the pearls of the collection. Such a circumstance comes back, for me, to that fact of my insuperably restricted experience and my various missing American clues—or rather at least to my felt lack of the most important of them all—on which the current of these remarks has already led me to dilate. There had been indubitably and multitudinously, for me, in my native city, the world "down-town"—since how otherwise should the sense of "going" down, the sense of hovering at the narrow gates and skirting the so violently overscored outer face of the monstrous labyrinth that stretches from Canal Street to the Battery, have taken on, to me, the intensity of a worrying, a tormenting impression ? Yet it was an impression any attempt at the active cultivation of which, one had been almost violently admonished, could but find one in the last degree unprepared and uneducated. . . .

For there it was ; not only that the major key was "down-town," but that down-town was, all itself, the major key—absolutely, exclusively ; with the inevitable consequence that if the minor was "up-town," and (by a parity of reasoning) "up-town" the minor, so the field was meagre and the inspiration thin for any unfortunate practically banished from the true pasture. Such an unfortunate, even at the time I speak of, had still to confess to the memory of a not inconsiderably earlier season when, seated for several months at the very moderate altitude of Twenty-fifth Street, he felt himself day by day alone in that scale of the balance ; alone, I mean, with the music-masters and French pastry-cooks, the ladies and children—immensely present and immensely numerous these, but testifying with a collective voice to the extraordinary absence (save as pieced together through a thousand gaps and indirectnesses) of a serious male interest. One had heard and seen novels and plays appraised as lacking, detrimentally, a serious female ; but the higher walks in that community might at the period I speak of have formed a picture bright and animated, no doubt, but marked with the very opposite defect. . . .

What it came to was that up-town would do for me simply what up-town could—and seemed in a manner apologetically conscious that this mightn't be described as much. The kind of appeal to interest embodied in these portrayals and in several of their like companions was the measure of the whole minor exhibition, which affected me as virtually saying : " Yes, I'm either *that*—that range and order of things, or I'm nothing at all ; therefore make the most of me ! " . . .

To ride the *nouvelle* down-town, to prance and curvet and caracole with it there—that would have been the true ecstasy. But a single " spill "—such as I so easily might have had in Wall Street or wherever—would have forbidden me, for very shame, in the eyes of the expert and the knowing, ever to mount again ; so that in short it wasn't to be risked on any terms.

There were meanwhile the alternatives, of course— that I might renounce the *nouvelle*, or else might abjure that " American life," the characteristic towniness of which was lighted for me, even though so imperfectly, by New York and Boston—by those centres only. Such extremities, however, I simply couldn't afford—artistically, sentimentally, financially, or by any other sacrifice—to face ; and if the fact nevertheless remains that an adjustment, under both the heads in question, had eventually to take place, every inch of my doubtless meagre ground was yet first contested, every turn and twist of my scant material economically used. . . .

As I wind up with this companion-study to *Daisy Miller* the considerable assortment of my shorter tales, I seem to see it symbolise my sense of my having waited with something of a subtle patience, my having still hoped as against hope that the so ebbing and obliging seasons would somehow strike for me some small flash of what I have called the major light—would suffer, I mean, to glimmer out, through however odd a crevice or however vouchsafed a contact, just enough of a wandering air from the down-town penetralia as might embolden, as might inform, as might, straining a point, even conceivably inspire (always where the *nouvelle*, and the *nouvelle* only, should be concerned); all to the advantage of my extension of view and my variation of theme. A whole passage of intellectual history, if the term be not too pompous, occupies in fact, to my present sense, the waiting, the so fondly speculative interval : in which I seem to see myself rather a high and dry, yet irrepressibly hopeful artistic Micawber, cocking an ostensibly confident hat and practising an almost passionate system of " bluff " ; insisting, in fine, that something (out of the just-named penetralia) *would* turn up if only the right imaginative hanging about on the chance, if only the true intelligent attention, were piously persisted in.

Put into my own much less luxuriant phraseology these passages simply mean that, throughout all his life, Mr. James has regarded the business life at least with curiosity and possibly with some small measure of awe. But I cannot believe, however much Mr. James might wish to hoodwink us into believing it, that our distinguished subject ever had any yearning to penetrate practically into the secrets of business life. And, indeed, let us take upon ourselves to throw down the glove that Mr. James, not being militant in any sense here upon earth, has been unwilling to throw down. Let us say boldly—for, indeed, in an Anglo-Saxon community it needs saying —that business and whatever takes place " down town " or in the City is simply not worth the attention of any intelligent being. It is a matter of dirty little affairs incompetently handled by men of the lowest class of intelligence. It can teach nobody anything and, if an immense cataclysm overwhelmed at once the whole of " down town " New York and the whole of the financial quarters of the city of London, in ten days the whole system would be running again, conducted by men of similarly mediocre intelligences. Of them this world contains millions and millions.

It is possible that there is something to be said for the actual manufacturer, the organising producer of cotton, wool, coal and the rest of the material products upon which our civilisation is based. And it is certain that a great deal might be said of the inventor of new processes, or of the man who actually and with his hands works in the mines, the mills, or upon the face of the earth.

The really producing classes have something to tell that is worth the attention of a man of intelligence, and so have the really leisured classes. The one may tell you what sort of an animal man becomes under the pressure of necessity, the other may tell you what sort of a being he will be when, the pressure of necessity being removed, he has leisure to attend specifically to those departments of life which differentiate man from the animal. And any other way of looking at these problems of our civilisation is the merest cant.

I am not, of course, writing a sociological essay, and I have said no more than is necessary to make, for my own immediate purposes, my own immediate point. And the fact remains as far as Mr. James is concerned, that Mr. James, if he has drawn a very perfect picture of one phase of occidental life, has done the greatest service that it is possible to do to the humanity of his day. If he has done this he has, in fact, shown us to what tend all the strivings of the men digging drains in the road, of the men setting brick upon brick in the building of houses, of the men toiling in the mines, of the inventors of new engines, of the clerks incessantly blackening pieces of paper, of the manufacturers organising the labourers of all these people, and of the business men, semitic or others who by the means of that most rascally of all forms of victimising — company promoting — take the profits of the labour of all us toiling millions. If Mr. James, then, has given us a truthful picture of the leisured life that is founded upon the labours of all this stuff that fills graveyards, then he, more than any other person now living, has afforded matter upon which the sociologist of the future may build—or may commence his destructions.

For, given that he has achieved this, the problem which will then present itself to the sociologist is no more and no less than this— are the prizes of life, is the leisured life which our author has depicted for us, worth the striving for ? If, in short, this life is not worth having—this life of the West End, of the country-house, of the drawing-room, possibly of the studio, and of the garden party—if this life, which is the best that our civilisation has to show, is not worth the living ; if it is not pleasant, cultivated, civilised, cleanly and instinct with reasonably high ideals, then, indeed, Western civilisation is not worth going on with, and we had better scrap the whole of it so as to begin again. For, you may by legislation increase the earnings of the labourer; you may by organising or by inventing increase the wealth of our particular Western communities, but what is the use of this wealth if the only things that it can buy are no better than are to be had in any city store—unless, along with material objects that it does buy, it gets "thrown in," as the phrase is, some of the things that were never yet bought by mortal's money. For it is no use saying anything else than that the manual labourer, if you give him four hundred a year and an excellent education, will have no ambition to live any otherwise, things being as they are, than as the dwellers in any suburb. And, supposing that you gave him a thousand a year he would, as things at present stand, have no other ambition than to live like one of the less wealthy characters of any one of Mr. James' books. There is no getting away from these facts in any Anglo-Saxon community, and even in France and Germany the tendency is much the same; though, of course, in both of those countries you happen upon such phenomena as farmers of very large income who continue to live the life and to wear the dress of farmers, without any thought of snobbishly imitating the lives and habits of suburban clerks or of hunting gentry.

So that the problem remaining to the sociologist, the politico-economist or the mere voter, after reading Mr. James' work is simply this : is the game worth the candle ; is the prize worth the life ? If they are not, then political economists must entirely change their views of what is meant by supply and demand, introducing a new factor which I will call the " worth whileness " of having one's demands supplied ; the sociologist must shut up all the books that he has ever read until he, too, has evolved some theory of what is worth while ; and the voter must insist upon the closing of all the legislatures known to this universe—until some reasonable plan of what they are all striving for shall have been arrived at. For the fact is that our present systems of polity and laws, being entirely based upon theories of economics, we have paid—none of us who are interested in public questions—any heed at all to the purchasing power of that money which by our activities we produce and which by our legislation we seek as equally as possible to distribute.

64

SUBJECTS

It is because Mr. James has so wonderfully paid attention to this question that I have advanced for him—and heaven knows he won't thank me for it—the claim to be the greatest servant of the State now living. Heaven knows too, that, things being as they are, it isn't much of a claim. For as greatness goes, looking at the world as it now appears, when was there ever such an amazing, such an overwhelming dearth of " figures " ? Where is the Bismarck of to-day, the dominating figure who balanced our whole world in one hand whilst he used the other for pouring down great draughts of mixed champagne and stout ? I heard the other day that there was a Bismarck of the Balkans. But this morning I read that he had been put in prison for peculation. Where is our Napoleon of to-day ? I know of a gentleman who advertises himself in public conveyances as the Napoleon of the roll collar for the City of London, but I know of no other Napoleon. Where are our Palmerstons, our Disraelis, our Lincolns, our Grants, our Stonewall Jacksons, our Emersons, our Carlyles, our Stephensons ? Why, even Mr. Pierpont Morgan is dead, and his, I think, was the last of the names with which you could have conjured through the whole world. So that it is not much of a claim that I am making for

HENRY JAMES

Mr. James—it is no more than saying that he is the only unbiassed, voluminous and truthful historian of our day. And, in our day, the greatest need of society is the historian who can cast a ray of light into the profound gloom, into the whirl of shadows, of our social agnosticism.

I do not mean to say that we haven't to-day historians galore, shoals of statisticians, whole heaps of philanthropic novelists, whole armies of Fabian pamphleteers. We have also Chancellors of the Exchequer in huge quantities throughout the Empire; there are several Reichs-Kanzlers in Europe, and I have not heard that there are any portfolios lacking holders in the Cabinet of the President of the United States. But all these things amount to nothing as far as any constatation of how we really stand is concerned. Our historians usually commence, like myself, as advanced democrats and, like myself, end as Papists and upholders of the Feudal system—at any rate, our historians are always trying to prove something, when they don't degenerate into mere machines for the collection of *Ur-Kunde*.

Our statisticians are almost invariably gentlemen with axes to grind either for or against some tariff or some social policy; our earnest English novelists are almost invariably, by some fatality, sentimental humanitarians with, in a public sense, an extraordinary number of axes to grind. Our less earnest English novelists remain recounters of anecdotes that are usually hardly even polite, or pathologists dealing exclusively in romantic exceptions. And our Fabian Pamphleteers — well, they are still Fabian Pamphleteers, members of the middle classes who try to force the working man into broadcloth clothes of their own particular pattern and into the employment of babies' bottles of their own particular make. Our Chancellors of the Exchequer—well, they are merely the opportunists of the moment, trying to force collectivist legislation upon an unwilling world when their particular party label bespeaks them individualists, or preaching individualist sentiments beneath a collectivist banner to audiences equally unwilling. As to the United States Cabinet— well, I know nothing about it ; but then, neither, I think, does anyone else outside Washington.

Now God forbid that I should be held as saying that any of our eloquent Chancellors, Fabian Pamphleteers, earnest and humanitarian novelists or upholders of the feudal system are in the wrong. They are probably every one of them absolutely in the right, and each of them would be the infallible saviour of

Society if only Society would listen to them, or if human nature could be kept from creeping in. But the point is that each and every one of them is a partisan of something or other— each and every one of the considerable figures, such as they are, of the world of to-day, with its confusing currents, its incomprehensible riddles, its ever present but entirely invisible wire pulling, and its overwhelming babble, its whole surface dominated by the waving of the halfpenny papers—every " figure " in the world is a partisan of some cause or other. Even M. Anatole France, who is a great, clear and negational intellect, is an anti-religious socialist, and to that end colours all his writings, observing like any other politician only that which he desires to observe. Mr. James alone, it seems to me, in this entire weltering universe, has kept his head, has bestowed his sympathies upon no human being and upon no cause, has remained an observer, passionless and pitiless like the narrator of *The Four Meetings*. As a writer, he has had no more sympathy for chivalrous feelings than for the starving poor. He just sits on high, smiling his sardonic smile and exclaiming from time to time : " Poor dear old world ! "

SUBJECTS

What then distinguishes Mr. James' picture of society—since I have claimed for it so high a quality of truth—from the pictures drawn by Walter Scott, Thackeray, Alexander Dumas, who is to all intents and purposes an English novelist, or, say, from the works of Charles Dickens or Charles Reade ?

Dickens was, of course, a propagandist, but, when he is engaged in propagandising, his work is so crude as to be almost beneath notice, and as much might be said for the late Charles Reade. Their novels aimed at the reform of definite institutions—the convict prison, the debtors' prison, the lunatic asylum and the workhouse. They took hard cases of institutions of this description, peopled them with characters all black, who perpetrated physical violences and other tyrannies upon characters who were white-hued as the angels are. They achieved notable reforms but, as writers, they were merely negligible in so far as the reforming passages of their works were concerned. A considerably greater skill in characterising is employed by the reforming novelists of to-day—by Mr. Galsworthy, Mr. Wells and other writers with purposes. But their works probably lose dynamic power as pamphlets on account of the art that they employ, whilst the value as documents is seriously impaired by the bias of their minds.

And these more modern writers are distinguished as coming after the distinct cleavage that is to be observed in the history of the English novel—a cleavage that began to be observed in the 80's and 90's of the last century. Roughly speaking, until that time the English novelist was a teller of stories more or less rattling in which the characters were as sharply differentiated into sheep and goats as, to take typical examples, Tom Jones is differentiated from Mr. Blifil, Tom Pinch from Uriah Heap, or Clive from Barnes Newcombe. Thackeray, of course, began to have some vague idea that a conventional villain may be a person quite as meritorious and much more heroic than the conventional hero. Therefore he could give you the figure of Becky Sharp, over whom he moralised in a brandyfied manner characteristic of the Georgian era —for Thackeray was a Georgian far more than a Victorian. But still, upon the whole, these were just stories—the stories of non-moral lives, lived by non-moral people. In order to give themselves dignity, both Fielding and Thackeray—and all their followers after them

—indulged in fits of moralising. This, since it was in solid chunks, the reader could conveniently skip in order to get on with the story. This tendency to buttonhole you, drag you into a corner and utter ethical rhapsodies, was the tribute these novelists paid to the public Anglo-Saxon belief that the reading of novels was a waste of time. Messrs. Thackeray, Fielding and school wished, as it were, to show that, although they were classed with mere tellers of stories like Scott, Lytton, Wilkie Collins, Harrison Ainsworth and the rest, they really when they got the chance could moralise as well as any bishop in any sermon, or as well as any Professor Ruskin, Mr. Carlyle and the rest of the Victorian prophets. Charles Reade and Charles Dickens, anxious also to assert the respectability of their professions, took upon themselves the jobs of reforming, as we have said, gaols, lunatic asylums and workhouses. When they had done this they could cry out : " Behold, we have cleared out these dark places in the land, we are no longer mere tellers of stories." And indeed they weren't — or indeed they were, according as their stories are skilfully or unskilfully told. But with the coming of the 70's, 80's, and 90's a new spirit began to percolate even into England. Into New Eng-

land it had percolated even earlier, because
New England with its centre at Concord,
Massachusetts, with its highly refined moral
atmosphere, its essentially Old English habits
of life and its New England conscience, which
is so much more a self-consciousness — New
England with its Emerson, its Holmes, its
Thoreau and, for the matter of that, its
Nathaniel Hawthorne, was in a much more
gentlewomanly frame of mind than ever
London, with its metropolitan spirit could by
any possibility be. Boston in fact, germless
and clean, was much more ready for the
inroads of a new cultural bacillus than ever
could be an old-world centre with its dark
places and its ungentlewomanly habits. The
new influence came much more in the shape
of Turgenieff than in the shapes of Flaubert
or George Sand ; for there is nothing in
Turgenieff that could bring the blush to the
cheek of any Boston gentlewoman. If you
will take the trouble to read excellent and
high-minded journals like the Atlantic
Monthlies of the seventies, you will be amazed
to find the immense influence that the " beautiful genius " must have had upon American
thought and possibly even upon American
life. You will find, particularly amongst the
important sections devoted to correspondence,

letters enough to fill volume after volume wherein the Boston young ladies asked imploring questions of the editor as to whether Bazarof was really a nice character, or even as to whether Liza should have given up Lavretsky. You will thus observe that New England, far earlier than England, began to concern itself with the real questions of humanity—which are precisely the questions as to whether Bazarof was really a nice character, and as to whether Liza really ought to have given up Lavretsky—far earlier than did the England which is on the eastern side of the Atlantic. And then, almost immediately afterwards, you begin to find the same young ladies writing their enthusiastic or imploring letters to the editor as to the ethics of Daisy Miller, or as to whether Madame de Cintré ought really to have given up the American. America was, in fact, ready to receive an even more dispassionate writer than was Turgenieff, and that more dispassionate writer was ready in the shape of Mr. James. It had, indeed, been ready for years before both for England and for the Western World in the figure of Anthony Trollope, who is a great figure too often forgotten. But Trollope, for reasons which I do not now wish to go into, was nearly as

much neglected in New England as were
those two other very great writers, Jane
Austen and Mrs. Gaskell. I don't mean to
say that America at large, at this period, did
not go on reading writers of the school of
Dickens and Thackeray or novels as portentous as The Mill on the Floss or Daniel
Deronda. But the hub of the universe had
succumbed to Turgenieff and to his disciple,
Mr. Henry James. Later, it succumbed to
Mr. William Dean Howells.

Mr. George Moore has somewhere cruelly
said that Mr. James came to Europe to study
De Maupassant, and that Mr. Howells remained in America and studied Mr. Henry
James. But a more exact rendering of the
statement would be that Mr. James came
to Europe and went about Paris in the society
of M. Turgenieff, whilst Mr. Howells remained
in New England and bathed himself in the
New England atmosphere with the New England conscience and all. (Mr. Howells, I
believe, resided, or at any rate resides physically, in New York; and the state of New York
is not, technically, a New England State.
But, though Mr. Howells' body may have been
physically somewhere up-town between Broadway and Fifth Avenue or somewhere down-
town in the neighbourhood of Franklin Square,

there can be no doubt that his soul was always on the Common, with its high avenues of thin-leaved elms, somewhere near the statue of that distinguished Englishman, George Washington, or at any rate between that statue and Trinity Church.) In the meanwhile, in England in the 70's there was no Boston for Turgenieff to devastate. There was, however, the Æsthetic Circle. These poets and painters were not so gentlewomanly and much less emasculated, and were beginning to lay claim to some of the intellectual tyranny that was exercised over the great Republic of the West by those refined personages with their atmospheres kept clean by the winds from Boston Bay. The English Æsthetic Circle never got so far as taking up Maupassant, who came a little later ; but Rossetti remotely and dimly perceived some of the qualities of Flaubert, and with some enthusiasm he acclaimed the greatness of Turgenieff. Turgenieff, both as a writer and as a man, was introduced into the Æsthetic Circle by a queer figure called Ralston, like Turgenieff, a gentle giant but of suicidal tendencies, who had lived much in Russia and who first translated a story of Turgenieff's—I forget which—into an occidental tongue. And in those days, for Rossetti or Morris or Swinburne to

" take up " writers was for those writers to be sure of at least a *succès d'estime*. Theo Marzials would talk about them and write about them, so would O'Shaughnessy, so would Oscar Wilde, so would Lady Mount Temple and so would a limited section of the Press and of society. In its dim and muddled way, intellectual England would be beginning to receive a new influence. And what was happening was really that the spirit of Richardson, which had crossed the Channel to light on Diderot, Chateaubriand, Stendhal, Flaubert and Turgenieff, was coming back to England, or if you like, that English intellectual life was coming back into the main stream of European culture. I remember that, as a boy, the books that I was told to read by my grandfather, who himself was a figure in the æsthetic society of that day, were firstly, of course, the poems of Byron—which I couldn't by any possibility read—and then Lisa, A Sportsman's Sketches, Fathers and Children, and, later, Stendhal's Le Rouge et le Noir and Flaubert's Madame Bovary. That would be in 1891.

But the European " influence " was as yet quite subterraneous. It was, as it were, practised in the cellars of the time, this reading of the works of the great Russians and the great French. For some reason or other, except for *Daisy Miller*, I do not think that the Æsthetics ever read much of Mr. Henry James, who had at that date been writing for about sixteen years. I am too young, of course, to say from personal observation how far Mr. James' fame had penetrated in circles non-æsthetic, but I should be inclined to say that, as far as he was concerned, the silver Thames flowed undisturbed and with no signs of conflagration. The great awakening of the 90's was heralded for him by the following episode, which I will leave Mr. James to recount.[1]

My clearest remembrance of any provoking cause connected with the matter of the present volume applies . . . to . . . an effort embalmed, to fond memory, in a delightful association. I make the most of this passage of literary history—I like so, as I find, to recall it. It lives there for me in Old Kensington days ; which, though I look back at them over no such great gulf of years—*The Death of the Lion* first appeared but in 1894—have already faded for me to the complexion of ever so long ago. It was of a Sunday afternoon early in the spring of that year : a young friend, a Kensington neighbour and an ardent man of letters, called on me to introduce a young friend of his own and to bespeak my interest

[1] Preface to Volume XV of the Collected Edition of the novels of Henry James, 1909.

for a periodical about to take birth, in his hands, on the most original " lines " and with the happiest omens. What omen could be happier, for instance, than that this infant *recueil*, joyously christened even before reaching the cradle, should take the name of The Yellow Book—which so certainly would command for it the liveliest attention.

It is not for me to state whether The Yellow Book was merely a land post on the edge of the cleavage that I have described, or whether it was both a land post and the wedge that drove itself in. It is certain that The Yellow Book gave a chance for publication, which didn't exist before and which has certainly never existed since—a chance for publication to really fine work of a high technical order. Technically, indeed, I should say that this periodical, which was so lacking in inchoateness as to be hardly a periodical at all but rather a periodically interrupted production of matter of permanent interest—this periodical represents the high-water mark of English achievement in the world of the Arts. Nothing that came before it was worth much attention from the serious critic, and nothing that came after it, if we except perhaps Mr. Henley's National Observer. However that may be, it is certain that The Yellow Book meant for the serious critic the end of having to pay attention to the botched and amateurish productions of the schools of Scott, Dickens, Thackeray, Reade, Dumas and George Eliot. I don't mean to say that the English " nuvvle " hasn't gone on being produced and being acclaimed by the English Press.

But the critic—who isn't compelled by the same trade exigencies as is the reviewer—has had, since 1894 or thereabouts, a small body of work produced which is up to a point worthy of his attention and which may at least legitimately excite his curiosity. Roughly speaking, before the 90's there was nothing at all—literally nothing at all except the novels of Trollope. Since 1894 there have been at times two or three, at times five or six, books a year to which someone of intelligence might turn his attention. You might, that is to say, without serious diminution of self-respect, read the works of Mr. Galsworthy, Mr. Arnold Bennett, Mr. H. G. Wells, of the late George Gissing. With reservations you might read those of the late Robert Louis Stevenson and the late George Meredith who, if they paid no particular attention to the architectonics of their novels or to the psychology of their characters —these being as a rule just as black and white as those to be found in the works of a Dickens

or a Reade—did at least pay some, if a quite
mistaken, attention to the potential qualities
of words. In a class quite apart as a serious
and conscious artist the critic would have to
place Mr. George Moore ; as a writer whose
personality has great charm but whose works
are not technically very interesting he would
await the books of Mr. Thomas Hardy. And by
themselves quite alone and above all others
he would put the books of Mr. Joseph Conrad,
Mr. W. H. Hudson and Mr. Henry James.

I don't mean to say that this is by any
means an exhaustive list. All that I am trying
to point out is that, for the critic, there is
some hope each year of finding a book or two
of interest produced by a writer in the English
language, a state of things that was impossible
before the 90's. Nowadays we may expect
in a novel, form and unaffected wording,
which are the things that interest the critic,
and some attempt at genuine characterisation,
and subjects which have some connection
with the real life of the day. They are, that is
to say, an attempt at shadowing the real
problems of the contact of individual with
individual. And it is because he was by so far
the earliest in the field, because his work is
so immense in bulk, so various in subject and
so intimately true to the life we lead, that Mr.

James, in the most literal sense, is to-day incomparable whether amongst novelists or historians. Mr. Hudson has a finer sense of words, Mr. Conrad is probably the more consummate artist, in the sense that he is the greater poet and has paid more attention to technical details ; but his stories deal so much less intimately with the normal products of our day that, in this particular department, he scarcely comes, Oriental as he is, into comparison with the great writer from the West.

Mr. James' work with its immense number of characters so amazingly rendered, so skilfully and dispassionately dissected and laid bare, is the exact mirror of the world as he knows it—of the world as we all know it. It contains without doubt the rendering of many hard cases—there is the American of the book called *The American ;* there is the lion of *The Death of the Lion;* there is Madame Merle in *The Portrait of a Lady;* there are the Colonel and his wife of *The Real Thing ;* there is Mr. Ruck of *The Pension Beaurepas ;* there is Kate Croy in *The Wings of the Dove;* there are the dependants upon the old lady in that most wonderful of all stories called *Europe.* There are in fact no end to the sufferers amongst Mr. James' characters, and we may doubt whether, during the extent of its par-

ticular " affaire," the artist who fails to find
employment for the two beautifully turned
out figures in *The Real Thing* isn't as much
to be commiserated for having them descend
upon him and so nearly ruin his work, as are
the Colonel and his wife who have to be sent
away. And so it is through the whole range
of this author's works. The normal novelist
presents you with the oppressor and the
oppressed. Mr. James presents you with the
proposition, not so much that there are no
such things as oppressors and oppressed, but
that, even in the act of oppressing, the oppressor isn't having a very much better time
than his victims. He does not, that is to say,
picture for you starvations, gaols, workhouse
wards, and slave-drivers brandishing whips.
That is not his business. His subjects in the
end are selected instances of long chains of
embarrassments, and his tragic note is rather
that of the nightmare than of the murder.
So that, when you consider the whole crowd
of his characters, you have, as it were, an
impression, giving a colour that is almost
exactly the colour of the life we lead. I don't
know exactly how many characters there are
in the thirty or so of volumes of fiction that
Mr. James has given to the world, but, from
Sir Jeoffrey Mandeville to Brooksmith the

butler; from Miss Bordereau of *The Aspern Papers* to little Miles of *The Turn of the Screw;* from Mr. Searle of *A Passionate Pilgrim* to the young lady who was the post-office clerk and heroine of *In the Cage*—there must be a thousand or so of them. There must be, major and minor, about as many people as the average man or woman will have amongst their acquaintanceship, their friends figuring upon their calling list or merely as their dependants. You have them all : the American tourists, some quite nice French people with titles, an Italian prince or so, the butlers, the housekeepers, the tweenie maids, the author or two and the artist or two, the large crowd of people in comfortable circumstances, a few peers, rather more peeresses, some journalists, some divorcees, and some of those vague figures in the background who are in the background of everybody's life, and of every garden party.

So that you have to imagine yourself in the very centre of the London season with its sense of an extraordinarily hurried but extraordinarily exciting rush through very peopled time, with its high skies, its boisterous winds, its ever present greenery of high trees and its equally ever present feeling that the end is approaching—that end which will see us all scattered from the moors to Silesia and from

Poitou to Rapallo, wherever our country homes or our châteaux may be. When, eventually, we get to those distant places, we shall have leisure to sit down and to reflect upon the season that is past and how, by it, we ourselves and everybody that we know will be affected in the season that is to come. But for the moment we are actually at one of the great garden-parties of the year. There is a band playing in the square ; the roadway is encumbered ; we hurry in because we have three other such places to go to in the course of the afternoon. But whilst we are waiting in the crowd of new arrivals for our names to be announced, we perceive Madame de Bellegarde talking to Milly Strether, whilst the Marquis gazes vacuously but still with a sinister expression at the conductor of the orchestra. Quite on the other side of the garden Newman is talking to Princess Casamassima, for though he has lost Madame de Cintré—who a little outrageously went into a convent—and although he has settled in London, he can't get away altogether from the attraction of titled continentalism. The author of Beltraffio is proving extremely boring to Miss Kate Croy, who can't keep her eyes off Morton Densher. Densher is actually in no danger at all, since he is only asking the mature

lady who writes as Greville Fane all about
the plot of her next play. He doesn't, poor
man, in the least want the knowledge, but he
knows how to keep a conversation going.
By one of those slips of an otherwise perfect
social secretary both Beale Farange and the
former Mrs. Farange had been invited to the
same party, whereas Beale ought to have been
asked to the one on the 4th and the lady to
that given in honour of the poor dear Mahara-
jah on the 18th. But there they are, the one
with his immense golden beard beneath
the tall plane tree in the middle of the square
talking to Mrs. Assingham : not far behind
whose back is that Prince of *The Golden
Bowl*—you never can quite remember his
name ; but you know perfectly well that he
very much wants to ask her some question
about the precise relationship of Mr. Verver
with the household of Poynton—or was it
Matcham ? Yes, certainly it must have been
Matcham. The former Mrs. Farange, with her
brilliant complexion, is being talked to by that
American chap, a tired and rather boring
enthusiast—you can't remember his name ;
but he was the chap who tried to get hold of the
Aspern Papers. You think he was even ready
to marry the governess. It was something
like that at any rate. The other American—

oh yes, his name is Winterbourne, and he
failed to marry that rather crude young
woman who died of Roman fever—Winterbourne
is talking to Count von Vogelstein who now,
with a harvest of ribbons, has retired from the
Diplomatic Service—talking about the real
motives of Bismarck in 1882. Just being
introduced to the notice of your hostess is
Lord Lambeth with Lady Lambeth, the very
model of a British Peeress, though she was
actually in a former state Miss Choate of
Milwaukee. You see, Lord Lambeth *had* in
the end to marry dollars, so that the Duchess
might after all just as well have let him have
Bessie Westgate. Miss Westgate married in
in the end that fellow—you can't for the
moment remember his name—who used to be
always everywhere because he was understood to keep a diary, but who hasn't been so
much about since his marriage. They never
are. But, by Jove—what an immense party
it is !—how jolly well our host does do them
when he takes it into his head to do them at
all. There *is* Bessie Westgate, and there is
Lord Lambeth, positively beaming straight
down upon her with his friendly smile. We
always liked her so much—and isn't she well
preserved !—we shouldn't wonder . . . such
things do happen. . . . But no ! Mr. James

wouldn't, at his party, have people who
could by any possibility get into such a
position. Of course the Beale Faranges are
there, but they were both such very old friends.
And then the incomparable Brooksmith is
upon you with his automatic : " What name,
Sir ? " and his equally inevitable : " Oh it's
you, Sir." In answer to a just breathed
question on your part, before he cries out your
name, he answers discreetly : " No, Sir, Lady
Barberina is not here yet. But Lady Agatha
Longstraw and Miss Maisie are in the dining-
room across the road. It's wonderful how
Miss Maisie do come on, Sir. You'd find Mr.
St. George in the dining-room too, Sir."
The incomparable Brooksmith can allow himself this moment of garrulity because your
hostess is taking a minute or two to talk to
Lady Wantridge about Scott Homer whom
she hasn't seen for so many years. But
Lady Wantridge goes, and you take your turn
for a moment before the high lady whose
relations with your host may be whatever
they are ; Mr. James has at any rate deputed
to her the task of receiving his thousand or so
of guests. And having heard her say, " Oh,
it's only you ; run, if you are capable of
running, in the direction of Mrs. Medwin's
pink sunshade which she certainly oughtn't,

87

poor lady, to hoist upon any such occasion. . . ."
You perceive quite close to the pink protec-
tion in question the tall figure of Mrs. Verveine.
Now how the deuce did Lady Euphemia know
that there was anything between—if there
possibly could in the most indefinite manner
of speaking be said to be anything at all—
between you and . . . ? But Lady Euphemia
knows positively everything ; she can see,
as it were, every one of the invisible cords that
runs between every one of the obscure couples
who so very obviously—so very carefully—
don't talk to each other but do talk almost
inevitably to somebody they don't in the
least want to talk to. And, for just a moment,
you have a sense of the immense strain, of
the immense pull of all the cords that such a
great London party means. You know to
yourself, as she knows to herself, how all
these people, beneath the high skies, amongst
the high trees of the square, drowning with
their not very loud voices the strains of the
discreetest of orchestras, smiling, moving,
appearing behind one group and disappearing
into another, you know the strain that is
upon them all, and the feeling that they all
have that this great function is no more
than an *étape*, a stage in the journey towards
an entire despair or towards a possible happi-

ness, that is always in such a low and such a tantalising key. But you put the thought from you as you walk (and you are painfully aware that it will probably be for the last time!) openly towards the figure that is beside the too palpable sunshade. Yes, it will have to be the very last time that quite openly you display at a party a really visible interest in the lady who now smiles so frankly at you. For you feel, boring into your back or at the very least tickling between your shoulders, Lady Euphemia's glance. And you know perfectly well that if you don't take a great deal of trouble you and Mrs. Verveine will be popped alive into one of those elegant volumes each of which is decorated by a photograph of Mr. Alvin Coburn's. For, after all, we too know a thing or so about some people; and don't we know that Lady Euphemia will tell every single thing that she observes to our distinguished host; for isn't she just no more and no less than the lady who in New York refused to go down town and in London averts her gaze from the Law Courts—isn't she, incomparable gossip that she is, just no more and no less than Mr. James' Muse?

Anyhow, that, for what it is worth, is the exact impression caused by the reading, for a matter of twenty-five years, the works of Mr. James. It is the effect of an immense concourse of real people, whose histories we just dimly remember to have heard something about ; whose figures we just dimly remember to have knocked up against here and there. Real! why they are just as exactly real as anybody we have ever met. The fictitious Prince von Vogelstein is just as actual a person to us as Prince von Metternich who was at the German Embassy only the other day, and Milly Strether is just as real as the poor dear little American cousin Hattina who faded away out of life twenty years or so ago. Nay, I will do the most profound, as it is the most humiliating homage, for what it is worth, that one novelist can make to another. On re-reading this morning, after an interval of perhaps twenty-five years, *The American*, I find that I have introduced, almost exactly as he stands in that book, one of Mr. James' characters into one of my own novels, written five years ago. You see, I first read *The American* during a period of my boyhood that was passed very largely in Paris, and very largely in exactly the same society as that in which Newman himself moved. And having read the book at the same time I really, twenty years after, thought that Valentin de Bellegarde was a young man that I had met somewhere in the society of the Blounts, the Goulds, the Uzès, the Saint Maurices, and the rest of that Anglo-Saxon society which was then beginning to touch hands with the dwellers behind the tall and silent porticos of the Faubourg St. Germain. Yes, indeed I thought that Valentin was one of my own connections whom I had liked very much. And so I considered myself perfectly justified in lifting his figure, with such adornments and changes as should suit my own purpose, into one of my own novels.

III

TEMPERAMENTS

WHEN an English firm, A, has occasion to write to an English firm, B, that Messrs B's representative has called upon them with an offer that does not seem attractive, they make the announcement in very much the same terms as those I have used. The American mind, however, is much more prone to allegorical or at least to figurative speech. Mr. A. meeting Mr. B. upon Broadway and narrating the incident would remark something like: "Your Mr. X. drifted in yesterday with a proposition; but we haven't no use for corner lots and battlefields, so we handed him a lemon and he quit."

The Englishman, in short, is almost incapable of calling a spade and spade. His language forbids it as well as his sense of caution. The American, on the other hand, making a virtue of the necessities of our common tongue luxuriates in a riotous symbolism. The Englishman falls back upon cliché phrases, the American soars into dizzy heights of inventive phraseology. So that, where the ordinary Englishman would write that Keats or Gautier lived always in the hope of writing " something that would pay," the extraordinary American—and after all it is only extraordinary Americans that will waste their time on anything so unprofitable as writing !—the extraordinary American will write of the aspiration in question as a " hope of successfully growing in his temperate garden some specimen of the rank exotic whose leaves are rustling cheques." And this is a very fine way of putting it, representing, as our distinguished subject might well say, one beat of the extended pinions that carried him so high in (as it were) the empyrean, and so far (as we all know) over the vast territory of the human heart. And let it be pointed out that this characteristic—which is, as I have said, a boldness growing out of a national shrinking— this characteristic is much more a part of the spirit of adolescent America than of ancient New England. Mr. James in fact began life in what he would call the last mentioned *parages*. And, having lived nearly all his life at a distance, his ear nevertheless has never done anything else but listen, amidst all the intermediate sounds, for any breath from that enormous Child. For if, physically, there have been few worse Americans, in the spirit there has not been a single better one. It is quite easy, in fact, to imagine Mr. James saying in the street of an English country town: " I think I observe a compatriot; let us go into this shop"; and into the shop we may very well imagine him forthwith bolting to avoid the contact. But this is far more Mr. James' tribute to Mr. James' own mental pose, one suspects, than his real desire. He doesn't, one imagines, in the least want personally to avoid anybody, even if they come from Falls River, New Jersey. The desire of his heart is to hear what they are doing in, or still more what they are doing to, Washington Square. He has longed, during all his residence in the Eastern world—he has longed as only the expatriated can long, for the latest news of General H. P. Packard, Miss Kitty L. Upjohn and Mr. P. C. Hatch, all of Brooklyn, N.Y.

But it has been necessary for Mr. James' immense process of refining himself, that he should keep away from the manifestations of the uncontrollable, and so very high-voiced, West. I have said earlier in this little study, that Mr. James has had no public mission in life. But that is only a half truth, if it is not an absolute lie. For, during the whole seventy years of his life which began in New England in 1843, Mr. James has had just one immense mission—the civilising of America. New England presented our subject with glimpses of what a civilisation might be. But you have only got to go to New England to-day to realise all that New England hadn't got, in those days, in the way of civilisation. You have only got to go to Concord, Massachusetts with its dust, its heat, its hard climate, its squalid frame houses, its mosquitoes, to realise how little, on the luxurious and leisured side of existence, New England had to offer to a searcher after a refined, a sybaritic civilisation.

I am not saying that there wasn't, between Salem and Boston, enough intellectual development to provide a non-materialistic state with fifty civilisations. It is obvious that you could not have produced an Emerson, a Holmes, a Thoreau or a Hawthorne—or for the matter of that a Washington Irving—without having a morally, an intellectually and even a socially refined atmosphere. Hampstead itself could not more carefully weigh its words or analyse its actions. But it would be fairly safe to say that, except for some few specimens of " Colonial " ware and architecture you wouldn't in the 60's have found in the whole of New England a single article of what is called *vertu*. If you will look at the photograph which forms the frontispiece of *The Spoils of Poynton*, in Mr. James' collected edition, you will see the sort of civilisation for which Mr. James must obviously have craved and which New England certainly couldn't have produced.

I must confess that I myself should be appalled at having to live before such a mantelpiece and such a *décor*—all this French gilding of the Louis Quinze period ; all these cupids surmounting florid clocks ; these vases with intaglios ; these huge and floridly patterned walls ; these tapestried fire-screens ; these gilt chairs with backs and seats of Gobelins, of Aubusson, or of *petit point*. But there is no denying the value, the rarity and the suggestion of these articles which are described as " some of the spoils "—the suggestion of tranquillity, of an aged civilisation, of wealth, of leisure, of opulent refinement. And there is no denying that not by any conceivable imagination could such a mantelpiece with such furnishings have been found at Brook Farm.

It was in search of these things that

TEMPERAMENTS

Mr. James travelled, as he so frequently did, to Florence where palazzi, and all that palazzi may hold, were so ready of access, so easy of conquest for the refined Transatlantic. In various flashes, in various obscurities, hints, concealments, reservations and reported speeches, Mr. James has set us the task of piecing together a history of his temperament. The materials for this history are contained in various volumes. There is, for instance, his very last production, *A Small Boy;* there are the prefaces to the volumes of his collected editions; there are his comparatively scanty collections of criticisms, the most important of which are contained in the volume called *French Poets and Novelists;* there is the life of Hawthorne; there are the books about places such as *A Little Tour in France, English Hours,* and *The American Scene.* It is therefore to these works that I shall devote my consideration for the space of this section.

A Small Boy, which is a touching tribute to the memory of our subject's brother, adumbrates the existence, mostly in the state of New York, of a young male child—of two young male children in a household of the most eminent and of the most cultivated. As far as one can make the matter out—as far,

that is to say, as it is necessary to make it
out for a work which is in no sense biographical
—Mr. James' father, Henry James senior,
was a person of great cultural position in
what is now called the Empire State. He was
not so much a representative citizen as a
public adornment. He was occupied in the
something like the reconciling of revealed
religion with science, which was then beginning to adopt the semblance of a destroyer
of Christianity. His published works were
numerous ; his eloquence renowned ; his refinement undoubted. For the matter of that
it was demonstrable, so that we have the
image of two small boys, whether in the
clean, white-porticoed streets of Buffalo or
of Albany, or in the comparative rough-and-
tumble and noise of a yellow-painted New
York that contained nevertheless at that date
gardens and pleasaunces. We have the impression of these two small boys of the 50's,
pursuing a perhaps not very strenuous, but
certainly a very selected, educational path
towards that stage in which William James
displayed all the faculty of analysis of a
novelist, and Mr. Henry James all the faculties
of analysis of a pragmatic philosopher.

And there is no doubt that there were
afforded to the quite young James—the small

boy—a quite unusual number of contacts with quite the best people. Figuratively speaking, not only did this particular small boy live amongst the placid eccentrics of New England but, in his father's house, he was exposed to the full tide that, running counter to the Gulf stream, from quite early days of the Victorian age, bathed the shores of the Western World—the tide, I mean, of European celebrities. I am not, of course, writing a history of American culture—though indeed a history of Mr. James' mind might well be nothing more nor less than that; but a very interesting subject lies open for some analyst in recording the impressions and adventures of the early tourists who entered on the formidable task of visiting, lecturing in, or, in whatever other intellectual way, exploiting the States of before the War. You will find traces of them in The Mississippi Pilot of Mark Twain where the formidable author tomahawks Mrs. Trollope, and several French and English writers who, having visited that gigantic but uninteresting and desolate stream, failed of seeing its snags and bluffs and steamer saloons eye to eye with Mr. Clemens. You will read the actual impressions of such a visit in Martin Chuzzlewit and in American Not s; or, in later American Memoirs

you will read of the disappointment caused
to distinguished hearers by Matthew Arnold's
faulty delivery of his lectures—his mumbling
voice, his frigid, English mannerisms. (How,
alas, one sympathises with the unfortunate
author of The Forsaken Merman !)

At any rate, lecturing and acclaimed, or
lecturing and appalled, and in either case
overwhelmed by that immense and blinding
thing, the world-famed American Hospitality
—they came, those pilgrims, in a steady
trickle. And it passed, that trickle, through
the house of Mr. Henry James, Senr., under
the no doubt observant eyes of Henry James,
Junr. It is not my business to particularise
who they exactly were—those great figures.
In order to catalogue them, I should have
to fall back on the record of conversations
with our subject ; and although I should un-
scrupulously resort to this, if it suited my turn,
it simply does not. It suffices to say that,
whatever may have been our subject's personal
contacts with Dickens, Thackeray, Arnold or
any other English celebrity to whom Henry
James, Senr., offered his fine hospitality, nothing
of their personalities " rubbed off," as you
might say, on to the by then adolescent
James—or, if anything came at all it was only
from the restrained muse of Matthew Arnold,

whose temperament, in its rarefied way, was as
" New England " as was ever that of Emerson
or James Russell Lowell.

To this coloured and contemplative child-
hood—I at least cannot discern in it any
traces of physical activities even so violent
as might be implied in the record of a game
of baseball—there succeeded an educational
pilgrimage to countries upon the eastern
verges of the Atlantic. Mr. James, that is to
say, studied one of the more non-committal
subjects—law, or it may have been philosophy—at a rather non-committal Swiss University. I use the phrase " non-committal,"
because it seems to me so very adequately
to express the institution itself, and not only
that, but its whole influence upon the career
of Mr. James. For, if our subject's *Mater*
had been *Alma* instead of *Respectabilissima*,
how different might not have been Mr. James'
range of subjects, though nothing, I imagine,
would have made much difference to his
temper. I mean that, if, instead of studying
law at Geneva, Mr. James had " taken "
the humaner letters at Oxford, Bonn, Heidel-
berg, Jena or even Paris, he might have
given us a picture of life much different,
though his sense of the value of what goes
to make up this troublesome career that,

somehow, we must get through, might have remained much the same.

It is not only along the lines of classicism. Classicism, it is true, has quite extraordinarily little part in Mr. James' pages. It is not, again, only that you will not find almost no mention in all the works (from *Roderick Hudson* to *The Finer Grain*), of Diana, Pasiphæ, Diodorus Siculus, Theocritus, or even of a writer whom, if he had ever mentioned him, Mr. James would certainly have called " poor dear old Euripides." . . . It is not, however, only that; it is that, right up to *The Golden Bowl*, in all the writings you will discern no trace of the Latin or Greek classical spirit. (I do not mean to say that there is no trace of classicality in all these singular and impressive works. It is, however, a Puritan classicism of a totally different genus.) But, even in *The Golden Bowl*, which we may regard as containing the maturest fruits of our subject's ripe philosophy, we have the singular remark that the banks of the Thames seemed, for the Roman prince, to have much more of the atmosphere of Imperial Rome than the banks of Rome's Tiber. And the singularity of this remark lies in attributing this imperialism not to the peoples but to the places.

God knows, the gentlemen who are responsible for the Embankment may be, imperially, more akin to those who built the baths of Caracalla than the monsters who were responsible for the modern bridge in front of the Castle of St. Angelo—as who should say that the spirit of the British Empire is more imperially Roman than that of the Kingdom of Italy. But even that comparison is singularly superficial.

I am of course well aware that our subject, in his careful impersonality, inserts that view of the Embankment into the psychology of a modern Roman prince ; so that he may well retort that that view does not in any sense represent his particular picture. But the whole spirit of his works speaks in that direction with no uncertain voice, and I cannot recall in any of his books of travel any directly countervailing pronouncement. It is, indeed, there, always a question of regions Cæsar never knew—in the spirit, though in the flesh he may well have there erected monuments.

Mr. James' is, in fact, a purely Protestant and a purely non-historic personality. (I am aware that I write a little as a black Papist and, for what it is worth, a Tory mad about historic continuity.) No one else could have placed a marble mantelpiece (it is one of Mr. James' rare betrayals of himself, that photograph !)

in a perfect specimen of a *Jacobean* manor house, and have invested the mantelpiece with such a veritable Jesuit's altar of gilding. They could not have done it and have called the results satisfactory to anybody but a collector.

But God forbid that I should be taken as grumbling at Mr. James for having so little, or for having none at all, of the historic sense ; for being so purely modern and so purely Protestant a product. His rendering, for instance, of Carcassonne, in *A Little Tour in France,* is archæologically inferior to any one-franc guide's ; but in its nice appreciation of surfaces and of forms it can do more for any visitor from Ilion, N.Y., or from Campden Hill, W.—than anything written by the hand of man about Carcassonne or any other place.

So the entire appropriateness of the " respectable " University on the banks of the lake as a place of study for the adolescent, contemplative and refined New Englander, shines out. At Oxford he might have studied the niceties of the enclytic δὲ in the Greek Testaments ; but he was so little of a schoolman that it would have done little for him. At Goettingen he might well have " taken his doctor " with a thesis upon verbal emendations in the various texts of Strabo ; but I cannot think that the spiritual geography of

TEMPERAMENTS

A Passionate Pilgrim would have been improved by the exercise. At Oxford, again, sociable soul as his writings bespeak him, he must have come as much into the social tone of the place as to have worn a rough pilot coat with huge buttons and to have acquired the art of driving a four-in-hand along the Trumpington turnpike [I know that that is " Cambridge "] ; at Jena, still sociable, he would have worn the high jackboots and dress sword of a chargierter and would have poured, as the habit there is, libations of beer over the bronze statue of the supposedly thirsty pious founder. But here again, I cannot imagine that the young James would much have enjoyed these activities ; neither would his books much have benefited. It is possible that into his views of English spreading lawns with decorative and highly intellectualised house-parties, strolling, seated, and always conversing upon them, he might have introduced figures engaged in pursuits more active, involving pellets more mobile than the purely conversational ones. But no pictures of country-house pursuits as they really are, no minute analyses of tennis, bridge, shooting or what you will could have atoned for a potential loss to the handling of what after all are Mr. James' true " subjects." No, in this, rather mutedly, best of all possible worlds; dominated by a blind Destiny Who nevertheless has a decent, almost a New England sense of the fitness of things, or at any rate of appropriateness —(so that if this particular Destiny does not move in any particularly mysterious way His wonders to perform, He at any rate sees that sobriety, continence and a general riding of the passions on the curb are rewarded by prosperity, the society of country-houses and the other things—still rather mutedly—worth having); in this particular best of all possible worlds the best of all possible Universities for our distinguished subject would certainly be Genf.

And I allow myself to discover in Mr. James, even at the latest epoch, a trace of—I won't say of affection, for the word would be ill-applied to this University that is *Mater*, not *Alma*, but *Respectabilissima*—a trace of remembrance of the respectability of this haunt of his contemplative youth. In the first version of *Daisy Miller* Mr. James lets his hero, Winterbourne, sit upon a terrace and look at a quite indefinite building that is Geneva University. But, returning to this story in 1909— it was first conceived in 1877—Mr. James obviously felt the necessity of treating his elderly Mater more respectfully and even more

tenderly. Therefore into the midst of his early
and dispassionate sentence he interpolates the
words : " the grey old ' Academy ' on the
steep and stony hill-side," thus claiming for
his early place of education, product as it was
of Calvinism, the hue and the quality of any
city of dreaming spires, home of lost causes,
and product—for in the end you cannot get
away from it—of Papists who loved learning.

Balzac we may take to have been our
subject's first serious literary model—or at any
rate his first conscious one ; and it is interesting
to consider how, at any rate on the surface,
in their late flowering and in their determination to produce contemporary history, the
voluminous author of the series of fairy tales
called the Comédie Humaine and the author of
the series of stories about worries and pertur-
bations resembled each other.

Balzac, I learn from the pages of Mr. James'
early study of his work—for I have never been
able to take sufficient interest in any other
of Balzac's manifestations than the Contes
Drolatiques to study very carefully his bio-
graphy or his bibliography—Balzac " before
he was thirty years old, had published, under
a variety of pseudonyms, some twenty long
novels, veritable Grub Street productions,
written in sordid Paris attics, in poverty, in

perfect obscurity. No writer ever served a more severe apprenticeship to his art, or lingered more hopelessly at the ladder base of fame."[1] . . . And if Mr. James, up till this very month in which I am writing, had not continued to manifest what is almost a reverence for Balzac, I should strongly have suspected him of writing those two sentences with his tongue in his cheek. For it is impossible seriously to consider that the turning out of twenty veritable Grub Street productions can be deemed—whatever else you choose to call it —an apprenticeship. At any rate, " before he was thirty years old," Mr. James had published to all intents and purposes nothing. That is to say, he had put out, firstly in the pages of a magazine and then in book form, a Balzac-Dickensian trifle called *Watch and Ward,* and in one of his prefaces he seems to hint that he published, here and there, various more or less fugitive trifles, before he had reached the fatal age for poets. And the first of his works that himself cares to rescue from oblivion— and we are dealing now only with the figure of himself that he cares to present to us—is *Roderick Hudson,* which was begun in Florence in 1874 (Mr. James being then thirty-one) and finished in New York, in East 25th Street.

[1] *French Poets and Novelists.* Macmillan, 1884.

TEMPERAMENTS

Again, from the Prefaces to the Collected Edition, we may gather that from twenty to thirty years of age our subject led, from one continental and English town to another, a drifting existence of hotels and of hospitality. They were, these visits, tempered with occasional returns across the water, in, as again we may gather, the rather desultory attempt to "take up" whatever profession it was for which his studies at Geneva had more or less qualified him. But, to all intents and purposes, our subject led what Catholics call the Contemplative Life, as severely withdrawn from the things of this world as any religious. So much at least we may assuredly lay down from the long passage I have already quoted relative to the attempts he made to induce his Muse to trot down town. And although the society of French cooks, governesses and the mistresses of drawing-rooms may strike one as, at first glance, a queer substitute for that of priors, sub-priors, almoners and primers, it is none the less, in a Puritan world given to attaching its greatest interests to the takings of railways, a substitute. It was, that gigantic up town cloister, at least a *milieu* in which, if you did not very much study the Sweet and Divine Nature, you had ample opportunity for studying all human manifestations—

at any rate, all that were separable from the acquisition of railway interests.

So that, in Florence, in London, in Paris, at Kew Gardens, Hampton Court, in haunts of ancient peace, show places and in New York, the states of Connecticut, Rhode Island and Massachusetts, we may imagine our distinguished subject, pursuing a modernly monachal life, tempered by the writing for the magazines of fugitive articles. He had, that is to say, secured his opening for delicate, temperate and contemplative prose in periodicals of the dignified and older order. We imagine him " sending in " papers on Florence, Kew Gardens, Hampton Court, the haunts, and upon any other places where the turf was smooth, the deer meditated beneath oaks and the sunlight lay upon mellow walls. There can be no doubt, when it comes to the reading of that touching—that yearning—story, *A Passionate Pilgrim*, that was published in 1875, there can be no doubt that our author had " tried his hand," had precisely served an apprenticeship of a full ten years, to what is called descriptive writing. For *A Passionate Pilgrim* is the apotheosis of the turf, the deer, the oak trees, the terraces of manor houses. It had never been so " done " before and never again will it be so done.

TEMPERAMENTS

Roderick Hudson, look at it how you will, is, in the scale of our author's work, the final example of 'prentice work ; *A Passionate Pilgrim* is the first masterpiece. Up till the year 1874 Mr. James was indeed serving an apprenticeship ; not the apprenticeship of turning out twenty Grub Street novels, but that real apprenticeship of living, observing, and occasionally trying his hand at a paper of prose for the older magazines. Mr. James, in the New York of that day, was already known as a personality not only of promise but of the certainty of performance. We might gather that—if we did not know it from the conversations of the master's early friends —from the statement in the Preface that *Roderick Hudson* was designed from the first for publication in The Atlantic Monthly. Of course an author might destine his work for The Atlantic Monthly—or for The Entomological Review—and the editors of those periodicals might turn it down. But *Roderick Hudson* actually began its serial publication before the story was complete, and it needs very little knowledge of the sapient editors of the older magazines—as of the newer, for that matter—to perceive that they would not " commission a serial " from a " hand " entirely untried. Here then is proof positive that in one magazine or another there must exist a considerable body of early work by our author. I am however so little—I conceive —concerned with it that I leave to some future aspirant for a literary doctorate the task of disinterring these prehistoric papers and, upon them, founding a thesis.

The fact is that *Roderick Hudson* gives so very completely the measure of the " earliest James." For our author was never a very exclusive artist in words—an artist, that is to say, in the sense that Flaubert and M. Anatole France are artists. Neither until after—until long after—he had written *Roderick Hudson* did our author become a master of plot, story, and motive, though his sense of form was always notable. Even until he had written *The Portrait of a Lady*, in 1879, we find that, if he did not think it essential to have villainous characters and heroic, oppressors and op- pressed, he found it at least highly convenient —thus you have the real villains, and mur- derers at that, in *The American*, and the villainous husband of the oppressed heroine of the *Portrait*—the villainous husband having by the still more designing Mme. Merle a real, tangible, illegitimate child.

That of course is Balzac—Madame de Belle- garde is Balzac—a wicked Balzac duchess.

TEMPERAMENTS

Madame Merle is improved Balzac—a Balzac adventuress brought a little nearer to the ground and a little rendered Anglo-Saxon.

In the Preface to *Roderick Hudson* we find, indeed, Mr. James at his confessions :—

To name a place in fiction is to pretend in some degree to represent it. . . . I had not *pretended* very much to " do " Northampton, Mass. . . . It was a peaceful, rural New England community, *quelconque* —it was not, it was under no necessity of being, Northampton, Mass. But one nestled, technically, in those days, in the great shadow of Balzac. . . . Balzac talked of Nemours and Provins : therefore why shouldn't one, with fond fatuity, talk of almost the only small American *ville de province* of which one had happened to lay up, long before, a pleased vision ?

Or again :—

The greater complexity, the superior truth (of the subject) was all more or less present to me ; only the question was, too dreadfully, how to make it present to the reader ? How boil down so many facts in the alembic, so that the distilled result, the produced appearance, should have intensity, brevity, lucidity, beauty, all the merits required for my effect ? How ? when it was already so difficult, as I found, to proceed even as I *was* proceeding ? It did not help, alas, it only maddened, to remember that Balzac would have known how, and would have asked no additional credit for it. . . .

HENRY JAMES

Thus you see how very explicitly *Roderick Hudson* was a piece of 'prentice work—that piece, as it were, that the apprentice offers to the attention of the world to show that he is ready to become, if not already a master, at least a very efficient journeyman. Indeed, in that latter passage, you may observe the apprentice is already beginning to discern that his master is, at any rate in certain aspects, if not wholly an amateur, at least a faulty practitioner. For, if Mr. James at that early age was maddened to remember that Balzac, with what is no more than a trick, would have turned the corner of the complexities of a given subject or of life, he must have been beginning to discern already the fact that Balzac, whatever else he may have been, was not in the least complex. He was, that is to say, on the way to make the discovery that he gave to the world ten years later—the fact that, in matters of the subtler contacts, Balzac was no more than the quack doctor at the fair of life. Or, to put the matter in Mr. James' own phrase[1]:—

This makes, it is true, rather a bald statement of a matter which at times seems more considerable ; but it may be maintained that an exact analysis of his heterogeneous opinions will leave no more

French Poets and Novelists.   1884.

palpable deposit. His imagination was so constant, his curiosity and ingenuity so unlimited, the energy of his phrase so striking, he raises such a cloud of dust about him as he goes, that the reader to whom he is new has a sense of his opening up gulfs and vistas of thought and pouring forth flashes and volleys of wisdom. But from the moment that he ceases to be a simple dramatist Balzac is an arrant charlatan. . . .

It is then no wonder that the young James, who was beginning to have visions of complexity and to have desires to cease being " a simple dramatist," should have found in his master little of a guide to his new developments. He had, in fact, with this book a sense of embarcation—a sense of embarcation into those seas in which, if the voyager finds no other pearl, he finds at least the uncharted land ; there, if again he is to survive his travellings, he must take life and his subject and humanity with its complexities, at least seriously. " He embarks, rash adventurer "— I am quoting the Preface again—" under the star of ' representation,' and is pledged thereby to remember that the art of interesting us in things . . . can *only* be the art of representing them. . . ."

It was at this point, then, that the temperament of our subject took its definite leave of

the 'prentice frame of mind as well as of its
subjection to Balzac. We find him, of course,
writing in 1884, " the attempt," of the Comédie
Humaine, "was, as Balzac himself has happily
expressed it, to *faire concurrence à l'état civil*—
to start an opposition, as we should say in
America, to the civil registers." And Mr. James'
self-consciousness being of so high an order,
one has little hesitation in saying that he too
must by 1884 have formed the design of
rivalling the Blue Books. He began probably
with no such settled ambition—but then so
did Balzac ; it is part of the remarkable,
superficial parallel. " We know not how early
Balzac formed the plan of the Comédie
Humaine ; but the general preface, in which
he explains the unity of his work and sets forth
that each of his tales is a block in a single
immense edifice and that this edifice aims to
be a complete portrait of the civilisation of his
time—this remarkable edifice dates from 1842.
(If we call it remarkable, it is not that we
understand it ; though so much as we have
expressed may be easily gathered from it. . . .)"
Isn't that passage—with its reference to
difficulties of comprehension of his hero's
preface, exactly what anyone writing of Mr.
James, his works and his Prefaces—above all
of his bewildering Prefaces—might set down ?

TEMPERAMENTS

But, by 1884, our subject had very obviously
arrived at a pretty precise valuation of the
pretensions of the master—of the shallow
places in his knowledge—of his absolute want
of any knowledge whatever. " He began very
early to write about countesses and duchesses ;
and even after he had become famous the
manner in which he usually portrays the
denizens of the Faubourg St. Germain obliges
us to believe that the place they occupy in his
books is larger than any they occupied in his
experience. Did he go into society ? did he
observe manners from a standpoint that com-
manded the field ?   It was not till he became
famous that he began to use the aristocratic
prefix; in his earlier years he was plain **M.
Balzac."** . . . " There is nothing to prove
that he in the least ' realised,' as we say, the
existence of England and Germany. That he had
of course a complete theory of the British
constitution and the German intellect makes
little difference ;   for Balzac's theories were
often in direct proportion to his ignorance. . . ."
. . . " If, instead of committing to paper
impossible imaginary tales, he could have stood
for a while in some other relation to society
about him than that of a scribbler, it would
have been a great gain.   The great general
defect of his manner, as we shall see, is the

absence of fresh air, of the trace of disinterested observation ; he had from his earliest years, to carry out our metaphor, an eye to the shop. . . ." I do not know that any more complete blowing to pieces of a revered master was ever perpetrated by the hand of man.

The fact is that Balzac was as complete a writer of fairy tales as the Brothers Grimm, Hans Christian Andersen or Brentano of the Hundred Soups, and, in the main, his financiers, duchesses and the rest, have no more relation to life—have much less relation to the life of 1850—than any adventurous tailor, bewitched charcoal burner or Rapunzel. The Comédie Humaine, except for César Birotteau, the Napoleon of perfumery, and for Père Goriot, the Lear of 1840 Paris, is a gigantic deception. Balzac had a certain—an even very intimate— knowledge of the Parisian lower middle class, of smaller money-lenders, of the lower ranks of churchmen ; and, had he limited his projections to these, his works would have had some value apart from whatever value may attach to fairy tales. In a sense he had some of the value of the pioneer ; he dimly perceived how the art of the writer of fiction might be redeemed from the slur that had been cast upon it by the very defects of which he possessed so liberal a share. And just as

Dickens, Thackeray and Fielding attempted to dignify their profession by appearing in the robe of the preacher, so Balzac, selecting the more valuable pretext—being by far the wiser charlatan—pretended to be at once a realist and a philosopher. Had he done what he pretended to do he would have been the most immense—as he was certainly the most industrious—figure of the modern world. But the fact is that, though he had got hold of a tremendous idea—an idea as tremendous as that of the railway, the electric telegraph, the Crystal Palace or the aeroplane—he was utterly without either the technical knowledge or the knowledge of humanity that would have carried it out. He knew less of either than Dickens, less than Fielding, much less than Thackeray, and he knew infinitely less than Smollett whom in many ways he resembled. But, if to all intents and purposes he succeeded not at all, he was of this inestimable service to humanity : he handed on to later writers that one great idea of their functions, the aspiration to *faire concurrence à l'état civil*—to beat the Blue Book out of the field.

And the first of all writers—the first at any rate of writers in the Anglo-Saxon tongue—to take advantage of this particular lesson of the master was our author. Let us consider what

were Mr. James' advantages. Perhaps the
first of these was that at an early age he had
read the line of Musset's : " Mon verre n'est
pas grand mais je bois dans mon verre " ;
perhaps the second was that he was a citizen
of the United States.

As regards the size of Mr. James' glass, I
have said almost sufficient. It was bounded
upon the one hand by his own temperament,
on the other by the human heart, and those
seem to me to be bounds sufficient for any
ordinary writer. I was talking the other day
to an active and intelligent Englishman—one
of His Majesty's ministers—upon this very
subject. He brought forward as a damning
indictment of our subject the fact that Mr.
James in none of his works deals with Politics,
War, the Lower Classes or Religion—with any
of the things that are properly written with
capital letters. I suppose that it is a sufficient
answer—not to report a desultory conversation
—to say that Mr. James knows nothing of
Politics, War, or the Lower Classes. Nobody
does. Nowadays all these things are so much
in the melting-pot of conflicting theories that
for anyone to dogmatise upon what would be
the outcome of, say, a war between Prussia
and France ; upon where the Liberal or any
other party will be in ten years' time ; or how

fittingly to deal with the Lower Classes—to dogmatise upon any of these themes that will so very efficiently settle themselves without any of our talking would be to write oneself down an ass indeed. It is true that that consideration will never hinder from doing so, myself or any other novelist, writer of leading articles, or pamphleteer. But it has hindered Mr. James, who is a wise man and who had the horrible example of Honoré de Balzac very much before his eyes in early life. As to Religion, that, in Protestant communities, is as it should be, very much in the melting-pot too. Mr. James, regarding the matter from an individualist standpoint, as all introspective Puritans must do, never really has it out of his mind. In so far as every one of his books turns upon an ethical point he may—in a Protestant community where ethics is so large a proportion and dogma so little, of Religion—be regarded as a purely religious writer. Indeed, occasionally, in such stories as *The Altar of the Dead, The Great Good Place* or *The Turn of the Screw*, he has permitted himself what he calls " indiscretions "—which implies that he has written stories that propagandise in favour of his particular interpretation of the Infinite.

But apart from these very few candidly labelled indiscretions, Mr. James has never committed the sin of writing what he "wanted" to write. For, if you ever chance to make, to an English novelist, any objections to parts of his work—to the way in which he has ruined the "form" of his works by dragging in digressions about erotics, humanitarianism, engineering or what you will, he will, your English friend, reply that he "wanted" to write it; as who should say he wanted to get it off his chest. That of course is a very relieving process for the novelist; as for the individual may be the practice of expectoration in public places. To the community, as to literature, it is death. The novelist is not there to write what he "wants" but what he *has*, at the bidding of blind but august Destiny, to set down. Not what he wants but what he *can*, finally and consummately, put on paper is the final duty of the writer. It is the measure of Mr. James' stern performance of his duty that he has never written anything more upon the subject of the invisible world than the two or three stories that I have cited. And the nature of those stories, the obviously high pressure at which they were written, the obviously strong emotionalism that inspires them, proves to us sufficiently what a lot our poor master had all ready to get off his chest. But it all remains a part of this great writer's private imaginings ; and the world is by so much the better—the better for the image of a great man who has greatly resisted a temptation that is more deleterious than drink, lechery, or any other of the cardinal sins.

Mr. James, then, has limited himself to writing of what he knows. And he has limited himself to writing about what he knows intimately and within himself. The ordinary writer—the Pre-Jamesian Anglo-Saxon, the Pre-Balzacian Continental, Balzac himself, I myself, and my friend Mr. Blank whose new work will be published on Monday by Messrs. Dash and Flutter—they, we, all of you, pretty nearly, do not so limit ourselves. If we are acquainted with the term " nine-cylinder, 160 horse-power, non-rotary Bréguet engine " and the fact—or perhaps it is not the fact—that a petrol engine running at high pressure develops the fumes of carbon monoxide or dioxide— given these facts we will, any one of us, undertake right away to provide you with the psychology of the driver of an aeroplane who becomes dizzy at ninety miles an hour and is dashed to pieces. We should also provide him with a lady friend to be dashed with him. That is the method of Shakespeare, Mr. Kipling, Mr. Wells, and whom you will, who either came before, or have not learned the lessons of, the Deluge. I do not mean to say that there are not some of us who will not be more conscientious in acquiring the details of the buzz, bang, rush, whirr, pull the right lever, order. But, roughly speaking, our method is to infer—to the measure of the deductive genius vouchsafed us—from a few spanners the whole body of an aeroplane, the whole psychology of the pilot. We try, that is to say, to infer what would be the feelings of a " chap " going through the air at ninety miles an hour —to infer them from what would be our own feelings as we imagine them to be likely to be. That is how Shakespeare produced the King of Denmark for our delight ; so that Hamlet's stepfather is of no interest for us except as a sidelight on the inestimable character of poor dear Shakespeare and is entirely valueless as a *document pour servir*, or as a guide to behaviour in the presence of a sovereign.

As regards the second of the golden spoons that Mr. James had in his mouth—I mean when he was born an American. . . .
There can be no doubt that this in itself is very largely responsible for his knowledge— apart from his mere surmises—as to the human heart and as to human manners. The position of the American of some resources and of

leisure was, in European society of the nine-
teenth century, one of a singular felicity.
Without, or almost without, letters of introduction or social passports of any kind, the
American " went anywhere." Anywhere in
the world—into the courts of the Emperors
of Austria as into the bosom of English county
families ! To know, or to admit an American
into your family circle, appeared to commit
you to nothing. There was the whole immense
Herring Pond between yourself and their
homes and you just accepted the strange and
generally quiet creatures on their face values,
without any question as to their origins, and
taking their comfortable wealths for granted.
Thus Mr. James could really get to " know "
people in a way that would be absolutely sealed
to any European young writer whether he
were Honoré de Balzac or Charles Dickens.
You can figure him (I am not in any way
attempting to do more than draw a fancy
portrait)—a quiet, extremely well-mannered
and unassuming young gentleman, reputed to
be very wealthy and in command of an entire
leisure, without indeed even so much tax on
his time as an occasional professional call in at
the Legation or ministry of his country. Still
he would be—he was—taken on the footing of
a young diplomat and, if he proved, on nearer

acquaintance, to be a thought more " intellectual " than one is accustomed to find in the young men that one meets in good houses, that was only part of a transatlantic oddness. Some oddnesses the amiable creatures must be allowed to possess, considering their distant and hazy origins ; you could be thankful if they did not sleep with derringers under their pillows—which they sometimes did—or pick their teeth with bowie knives.

Thus we may consider that Mr. James, starting upon his European career, came in, at once, upon the very top. If he had been an English writer he would have been at it twenty years before he knew an English countess ; he would die without having exchanged ten words with the wife of a duke, just as Balzac died without having had a glimpse of an interior of the Faubourg St. Germain. But that street of high walls had no terrors for Mr. James, and if his Madame de Bellegarde in some ways resembles a Balzac Marchioness, that is much more owing to the hold that Balzac and his methods had over our subject's imagination than to any want of social knowledge. Mr. James, I mean, knew perfectly well that the matrons of the most corrupt of European aristocracies do not go murdering their husbands in order to secure eligible *partis* for their daughters. That is just a proceeding out of the fairy-tale realm of the Comédie Humaine. And indeed the whole machinery of the murder is amusingly handled. You can see the young James boggling at an actual poisoning so that the Marquis, from what one can make out of the episode, died at a look from his atrocious wife. Just imagine a *vieux marcheur* of a marquis, cynical, improper and given in addition to intrigues with housemaids, fading out of life presumably because he learns from a look that he has lost his wife's affections, for all the world as if he had been the New England heroine of a sentimental tale! Mr. James, even at that early date, knew better as far as Life was concerned; but his comparative inexperience in the construction of novels led him into the paths of staginess. His desire was to give us the problem of what an aristocratic family would do when faced with a transatlantic gentleman with some sort of a " hold " over them. His invention went, however, at that date, no further than a " letter "—a veritable *patte de mouche*—at which the most craven of aristocrats would have roared with laughter. Nothing, indeed, could well be more comic than to observe how the Muse of our subject, who even at that date was a delicate and contemplative young lady, minces around and refines upon this portentous subject which Mr. James tyrannously presented to her, for all the world as if she had been presented with the task of ending the story of the proud Lady Dedlock and her disagreeable past.

But the change came soon enough ; soon enough we find Mr. James beginning to listen to the voice of the lady who was so faithful to him through life. She made herself heard with her not loud, but distinct and persistent, organ long before even *The American*—not to mention *The Portrait of a Lady*—was under way.

Mr. James' bibliography is a little difficult to follow, but, as far as I can make it out, *Madame de Mauves*, *A Passionate Pilgrim* and *The Madonna of the Future* were written immediately after *Roderick Hudson* and immediately before *The American*. In these three stories our master was beginning to find himself.

If it is obvious it is none the less significant that, whereas our subject's novels remained until a latish date by comparison—but only by comparison—crude, his very earliest short stories have a quality of vague fragrance, of indeterminateness, of charm. I can imagine several reasons for this.

TEMPERAMENTS

In the first place, there is the reason prudential. In the seventies of the last century anything in the nature of an exploring of one's temperament, and an exploiting of it, was no mean experiment. The dogma that it was necessary to have a story, " with a beginning, a middle, and an end " all complete, was hardly then doubted. It might be the story of a scrap of paper; it might, as in the case of *The Portrait of a Lady*, turn round no more than the wicked husband and the femme incomprise, but " plot " there must be. Now to pin on to a mere experiment the immense labour, the long lapse of mere time, that go to the writing of a full-dress novel would be a very rash proceeding—and Mr. James was never the person to be rash. He would, in the nature of things, prefer to confine his desire for writing studies to his shorter flights.

Secondly, we have to consider that, whatever he may or may not have otherwise been, Mr. James is—and was from the first—the great master of the *nouvelle* in the Anglo-Saxon tongue. This form (which is to the ordinary " plotted " short story what *vers libre* is to the sonnet) can only be called in English the longish-short story—or the longish-short sketch. You do not find in it the economically worded, carefully progressing set of apparently discursive episodes, all resolved, as it were, in the *coup de cannon* of the last sentence, that are found in one of the *contes* of Maupassant; nor, on the other hand, is it a short novel like Paul and Virginia, The Vicar of Wakefield, or Colomba. It is rather no more and no less than the consideration of an " affair." The whole of the story, of the murder, of the liaison, of the bequest, might well be related in the opening of the first paragraph.

The author might then devote the whole of the rest of the " action " to the consideration of the mental states of the various characters affected. I do not mean to say that he must do this; still less is the Anglo-Saxon novelist to be allowed, as he is perpetually trying to do, to escape from the claims of " form " under the pretext that he is writing a *nouvelle*. The " form " of this type of production, like the form of *vers libre*, is infinitely the more difficult simply because it is the more undefined. That, however, is a matter to which I shall return. What I am mainly concerned with here is the fact that the *nouvelle* appears to offer unrivalled scope for the development of one's temperament and that in it—in *A Passionate Pilgrim* as in *The Madonna of the Future* ; in *Daisy Miller* as in *The Four Meetings*—Mr. James for many years had all the appearance of developing his.

TEMPERAMENTS

This brings me at once to the consideration of Turgenieff, though I am aware that it never takes much to do that. I am still not concerned historically with exactly when our subject came across the beautiful genius mentally, or with the precise date on which he met him in the flesh. But the very first meeting with a *nouvelle* by the Russian writer must have been a wonderful eye-opener for our master. It must wonderfully, I mean, have shown him " what could be done " by, let us say, a contemplative and leisured young New Englander, wandering desultorily across Europe and privileged to hear the gossip of the best people. For admission into European—into any—society means no more and no less than the privilege to hear its gossip, to receive some of the confidences of matrons as to their worries about their daughters, to be privileged to hear some of the real, private views of the men folk as to certain others of their sex. This New Englander, thus wandering and thus privileged, and above all loving (and being able to use) gossip as no one else ever loved or used it—this happy prince, Mr. James found himself to be. And, if the beautiful genius had not yet taken hold of him, there could not be any doubt that in the early seventies our distinguished friend was peculiarly in a state of grace—was pecu-

liarly open to the ravages of that particular
bacillus.

I think that in two quotations from one of
our author's prefaces I can give you the whole
of this one side of his figure. This is Mr. James
writing in the summer of 1873, the story called
Madame de Mauves :—

I recall the tolerably wide court of an old inn at
Bad-Homburg in the Taunus Hills—a dejected and
forlorn little place (its *seconde jeunesse* not yet in
sight) during the years immediately following the
Franco-Prussian war, which had overturned, with
that of Baden Baden, its altar, the well-appointed
worship of the great goddess Chance—a homely
enclosure on the ground level of which I occupied a
dampish, dusky, unsunned room, cool, however, to
the relief of the fevered Muse, during some very hot
weather. The place was so dark that I could see my
way to and from my inkstand, I remember, but by
keeping the door to the court open—thanks to which
also the Muse, witness of many mild domestic incidents, was distracted and beguiled. In this retreat
I was visited by the gentle Euphemia ; I sat in
crepuscular comfort pouring forth again, and no
doubt artfully editing, the confidences with which
she honoured me.

And isn't it just precisely after such a visit
of his lady that Mr. James may have got up
and strolled amidst the shaded paths around

the pump-room—the paths across which nowadays the golf balls fly ? And, strolling decorously, must he not have met another decorous stroller, he listening with his sweet, sad, enigmatic smile to the confidences of Princess P—— who would be upon his right arm, and at the same time to those of landed-proprietor W——ff who would be grumbling into his left ear ? Can't we imagine, in fact, that, strolling at such a pace, in much such a season, in that sort of place and frame of mind, in the contemplative and respectable seventies, our author first met the beautiful genius ? Let me once more hasten to say that this is only an imaginary picture of what might have happened, Turgenieff having been much at Nauheim, Homburg and similar places of sad or agreeable loungings. It would not be even necessary to postulate that our author ever met the Russian writer ; Turgenieff was in those days so much in the air, and the air then was so exactly suited to his frame of mind and so ready for his pervasion, that no actual meeting would have been in the least necessary. Mr. James would have had " to go about with " the beautiful genius, if not in his actual company, in Paris, in Florence, on the Taunus Hills or in the haunts of ancient peace—he would have had to have Turgenieff with him, if not at his side, then, in his head, in his heart, in his pockets, in his portmanteau.

That then was the early James, in his chastened, rarefied, not yet quite European habit. Let us take a picture of him in his more luxuriant robustness, in his full strength, as nearly pagan as it was possible for one to be who was born under the shadow of Brook Farm or of Concord in its entirety. Mr. James is speaking here of how he got hold of the " subject " of *The Reverberator* that was published in 1888.

" It was in a grand old city of the south of Europe (though neither in Rome nor yet in Florence) long years ago, and during a winter spent there in the seeing of many people on the pleasantest terms in the world, as they now seem to me to have been, as well as in the hearing of infinite talk—talk, mainly, inexhaustibly about persons and the personal equation and the personal mystery. This somehow *had* to be in an odd easy, friendly, a miscellaneous, many coloured little metropolis, where the casual exotic society was a thing of heterogeneous vivid patches, but with a fine old native basis. . . ."

Between, however, the chastened, comparatively reticent days and this luxuriance of phrase and of gossip as well—between these two phases there went a whole mint of developments. This we might well call the frame of mind of *A Little Tour in France :* this developed later into the frame of mind of *The American Scene* which again and later still was to become the mystifications and bewilderments of The Prefaces, those wild debauches.

But, in between the circumstances of *Madame de Mauves* of 1873, and the writing of *The Little Tour*, we have to place—as it helps us to place our subject—the collected papers of the volume called *French Poets and Novelists*. The volume was published in England in 1884, but the papers, as far as their writing was concerned, had been scattered through several previous years. In this volume our author desperately belauds Balzac, places Turgenieff at the top of the tree, damns Flaubert—whom he always disliked—poor dear old Flaubert !—by bracketing him in the same paper with Charles de Bernard, an, even then, forgotten scribbler who hopelessly imitated but in some respects improved upon Balzac. He writes about Musset with great justice and very little sympathy ; about *ce pauvre* Théo with a great deal of sympathy and not much critical justice ; about George Sand with relish as a wicked old woman, and about

135

Mérimée with pity for his physical ills and
with not much feeling for his clear, hard
diction.

French Poets and Novelists is, in fact, much
more—however skilfully Mr. James sought to
veil the fact—an expression of likes and dis-
likes than a display of criticism, criticism
dealing with things by a certain standard and
leaving liking to take care of itself. That does
not make the volume any less valuable as an
index to our present study—the development
of Mr. James' temperament. As such it is
just simply of the highest order.

To write of L'Education Sentimentale—that
illuminating work of which someone has said
that even to begin to understand it you must
read it fourteen times—and I, I who speak to
you, have done that and affirm the truth of the
other writer's statement—to write of this book
thus :—

" . . . To read it is, to the finer sense, like
masticating ashes and sawdust. L'Education
Sentimentale is elaborately and massively
dreary. That a novel should have a certain
charm seems to us the most rudimentary of
principles, and there is no more charm in this
laborious monument to a treacherous ideal
than there is interest in a heap of gravel "—
such writing is the merest petulance, the merest

vexation. The vexation was not without cause —for L'Education Sentimentale is, in its own self, that real Comédie Humaine that Balzac professed to have written ; and it is vexing to find that a real person has come along to do what one's pet charlatan has only professed to perform.

Or again, such an *obiter dictum* as this, introduced into an article upon Charles Baudelaire whom our author much disliked : " Baudelaire was a poet, and for a poet to be a realist is nonsense "—to read such a sentence !— makes one despair of human nature. But the fact is that our master was at that date a revolutionist of letters who, coming from New England in search of the Finer Sense and the Finer Reticence of Europe, much disliked what he found. Mr. James was in the same boat as Flaubert and Baudelaire, but his dislike for their figures in its expression was unbounded. Flaubert looked at life with all its dirt, its treacheries, its accepted ideas and, by rendering them to the life, might well have driven them out of existence. Mr. James also has looked at life with its treacheries, its banalities, its shirkings and its charlatanries, all of them founded on the essential dirtiness of human nature,—*qui vous donne une fière idée de l'homme !* Like Flaubert, he has rendered these tendencies of his fellows, but with a more delicate irony ; and, if the world read him to any great extent, the world might well be a pleasanter place.

Yes, Mr. James was in the same boat with Flaubert, with Zola, with Turgenieff, with Maupassant, even with Baudelaire. But, since he had come to Europe to find respectability, he tried desperately to ally himself with the comparatively established Balzac, Sand, Charles de Bernard. One expects him almost, in these manifestoes, to enthrone Dumas Père, and all his contemporaries—the aristocratic Turgenieff alone excepted (though even the beautiful genius whom he sets on a level with *George Eliot !* was to be reproached, according to our author, with " delighting in sadness "). All his other contemporaries of any significance our author shrinks from. If it would be too much to say that this suggests to us the figure of Satan rebuking sin, at the very least it must suggest the elegantly habited form of a Robespierre animadverting on the dress, habits and aspirations of Danton, St. Just, Maillard and Couthon.

The real fact is this : The volume called *French Poets and Novelists* is, before anything, the first expression of a gigantic disappointment—the first formal confession of all the young James' *illusions perdus*. It is impossible to imagine that Mr. James was ever even relatively *naïf*; yet, at the cost of scrupulously investigating, we find the impossible imagination become the indubitable fact. There is a passage in *A Passionate Pilgrim* that puts the matter exactly enough—and all the more exactly because our subject, in his later revision, has very efficiently—and with a mature and bitter irony, crossed the "t's" and dotted every "i." For, if this is what the fictitious Passionate Pilgrim came to find in Europe, isn't it what Mr. James, a pilgrim just as passionate and by now much more hopeless, so vainly sought ?

It was my thought that I believed in pleasure here below; I believe in it still, but as I believe in the immortality of the soul. The soul is immortal certainly—if you've got one ; but most people haven't. Pleasure would be right if it were pleasure right through ; but it never is. My taste was to be the best in the world : well, perhaps it was. . . . I think I should have been all right in a world arranged on different lines. Before heaven, sir—whoever you are—I'm in practice so absurdly tender-hearted that I can afford to say it : I entered upon life a perfect gentleman. I had the love of old forms and pleasant rites, and I found them nowhere—found a world all hard lines and harsh lights, without lines, without composition, as they say of pictures, without the lovely mystery of colour. . . . Sitting here in this old park, in this old country, I feel that I hover on the misty verge of what might have been ! I should have been born here, not there ; here my makeshift distinctions would have found things they'd have been true of . . . This is a world I could have got on with beautifully.

Thus the Passionate Pilgrim, sitting in no place further to seek than Hampton Court— this poor American, with all his *naïveté* still virgin, voices what is the final, sad message of Henry James to humanity. Or perhaps the last words of *The Madonna of the Future* may enshrine the final message : " I seemed to catch the other . . . echo : ' Cats and monkeys, monkeys and cats—all human life is there.' " But that is perhaps too much of an echo of the Beautiful Genius to be true James ! No, I prefer " *The soul is immortal certainly—if you've got one ; but most people haven't ! Pleasure would be right if it were pleasure right through ; but it never is.*" And this, you will observe, is the gentleman who reproached Turgenieff with delighting in sadness, Flaubert with cynicism, and Baudelaire with loving dirt !

But that was in the early eighties when some of our subject's illusions still remained.

I have said that the conscious or unconscious mission of Mr. James was to civilise his people—whom he always loved. To put it more exactly, now that we have a little developed our theme, we should say that our author's mission in coming to the Old World was to find a *milieu,* an atmosphere, upon which America might safely model hers—an atmosphere in which wise and sympathetic duchesses and countesses said always the right thing, observed the " old forms and pleasant rites," an atmosphere half that of Florence, half of Hampton Court with a flavour of Versailles. From Italy, France and England the dayspring was to have come ; but half a century of pilgrimages have left him with no further message than that—that the soul's immortal, but that most people have not got souls—are in the end just the stuff with which to fill graveyards ; that *cela vous donne une fière idée de l'homme; homo homini lupus,* or any other old message of all the old messages of this old and wise world. Bric-a-brac, pallazzi, châteaux, haunts of ancient peace—these the pilgrim found in matchless abundance, in scores, in hundreds. Poynton, Matcham, Lackley, Hampton. . . . " The gondola stopped ; the old palace was there. How charming ! it's grey and pink. . . ." From the first visit to Madonnas of the Louvre, in

The American, to the last days of the epony-
mous vessel of *The Golden Bowl,* there is no
end to the *articles de vertu.* . . . But as for the
duchesses with souls—well, most duchesses
haven't got them !

Italy gives you as her final figure the Prince
of the last novel—a person not much different
from any American ; England gives you, as
the coping-stones of its haunts of humanity,
Beale Farrange, the child bandied from pillar
to post ; the Gereths, mother and son—
brigand or imbecile ; and the Brigstocks.
And France—well, as France would—France
first knocked the stuffing out of our poor
master's Utopia. . . . For, from New England
the young James had looked upon Europe as
a place where Balzac and George Eliot were
worshipped in an atmosphere of old forms and
pleasant rites. And in France he found
Revolution—an atrocious figure of a sort of
berserker in a dressing-gown who was banging
down all the pillars of all the old academies
and roaring out "*A bas*——*!*" well, down with
accepted ideas !

It was not, in fact, rest, amenities, serenities
—other than in title—standards, rites, or
anything settled, that Mr. James was to find
in Europe. . . . It was rather the shaking off
of academicisms ; he left far more respect-

ability behind him, in New England. And the final knock came from an Empire of which New England might well never have heard— New England which cherished its reasoned optimism ; its belief in a Destiny that gives a chastenedly good time to the sober, the industrious, the continent—to those, in fact, that bridle, self-consciously, their passions. . . .

That virus we may see already working in so early a book as *The Portrait of a Lady.* There, the self-conscious, self-bridling New England heroine ensues a lifetime of yearning misery at the hands of a possibly exaggerated, but still quite possible, pair of selfish scoundrels, so that Providence fails of its mission. . . . No, the writer who, acting by the standards of New England, in 1884, reproves the Russian author for delighting in sadness, could very soon give Turgenieff several points and a good beating. For the Russian could never have written *The Turn of the Screw ;* and, if he could have given us *Daisy Miller,* he certainly could not have written : " Cats and monkeys, monkeys and cats—all human life is there. . . ." At the end of one of the Russian's books a character is left, sitting gazing enigmatically into space and wondering if Russia will ever produce a Man. But what Mr. James wants is a civilisation—and just

143

because the American's aspirations are bound-less by comparison, so his final note is despair. Turgenieff's is only an enigmatic sadness. . . .

That is the nett result. As to the stages of despair I have not the space—I have not indeed the inclination—to pursue them very minutely. . . . We have the decidedly continental Mr. James who continued until the early eighties, ending perhaps with *A Little Tour in France,* in which perhaps he was taking a farewell conscious or unconscious of Latin ideas. We have the international frame of mind, as our author calls it—a phase which produced *The Four Meetings, An International Episode, The Pension Beaurepas, The Siege of London, Lady Barbarina* — a phase which lasted, let us say, for four or five years with occasional revivals. We have what Mr. James calls the " Kensington days " which produced the wonderful studies of English authors and artists with their infinitely saddest of all lives led by mortal man. Those days of contact with the wonderful Yellow Book group gave us that wonderful series of stories—*The Death of the Lion, The Lesson of the Master, The Next Time, The Real Thing, The Coxon Fund, Greville Fane*—and just as the wonderful periodical was the only place in which these stories could have appeared, so our wonderful master was the only man who could have given us those *nouvelles*. I harp so upon the word wonderful because I find literally nothing to say about these things—I have just wonder, and that is all that there is to it. . . .

And then, in what it is convenient to label the Rye days, our master gave us firstly the final masterpiece—I don't mean the last, but the most consummate—in *The Spoils of Poynton*. It was as if, with the failure and passing of The Yellow Book and of the Yellow group; with the extinction of the last attempt at an establishment of a literary and artistic life in England—with the passing of the glorious early nineties, Mr. James gave up the attempt to make an artistic *milieu* interesting to the inhabitants of this island. The first and only attempt! There is no doubt that it was another disillusionment. . . .

Our subject had tried to find in London, in English society, a region, or at least a corner, in which the only really productive class (of all the classes and all the masses) might be, if not honoured, then at least allowed some social value, even if it were the barest of social existences. But, with *The Death of the Lion* he had seen to the bottom of that possibility. A master, as he seems to tell us, might have a chance of an invitation to an " English

145

country house," but only on condition that he was a Lion. And then he would have to compete with Guy Walsingham, the lady novelist with a male pseudonym, and with a moustached wonder writing under a lady's name ; and he would, the master, be allowed no fire in his bedroom and would die of pneumonia in such a way as to get the hostess great credit in the Press for having afforded the master a room in which to die. . . .

So that, giving up this attempt to paint a life which is no life—(since in England the author, as such, ranks beneath the governess and the vicar and just above the servants, has no canons, no costume, no habits as a class and no rank in the State, and it is impossible to make " atmospheric " studies of a life where there are no habits, no costumes, no manners, no canons, no standard, no solidarity, no aims, and no rank in the State !)—giving up this impossible attempt Mr. James devoted himself to the task of portraying the lives of English people who were just people—good people, comfortably off, as a rule. He had tried to find his Great Good Place—his earthly Utopia —in Italy, in France, in English literary life. He had failed.

He found English people who were just people singularly nasty. For he gave us *The*

Spoils of Poynton, a romance of English grab ; *What Maisie Knew,* a romance of the English habit of trying to shift responsibility; *The Turn of the Screw,* a romance of the English habit of leaving young children to the care of improper maids and salacious ostlers ; and so on, right up to *The Golden Bowl* and *The Bench of Desolation,* neither of which could be called exactly " pretty " stories, though the latter is cheerful by comparison and in a desolating way.

So that it was not there, I imagine, that he found his Place. It was—again I imagine—in desperation that, quite late, he essayed a pilgrimage amongst his own people. This was probably foreshadowed in *The Golden Bowl,* which was another international story, re-introducing American characters. It is difficult to say how much Mr. James enjoyed the American Scene ; the splendid product is there for examination ; but I will hazard a small fortune in a bet that our author, if he did not find the average American any whit less desirable or less civilised than the average European, brought away nothing that could shake his conviction that most people have not got souls. . . .

Therefore we have the image of the Great Good Place—that only real castle in the air,

that ever-unattained and ever-waiting region,
beyond the frontiers of every horizon, the place
that, when our eyes are weary and when we
shut them, we may imagine. Of that place
indeed—but it is not in Europe—Mr. James
may say with his Pilgrim :—

" Sitting here, in this old park, in this old
country, I feel that I hover on the misty verge
of what might have been. I should have been
born here, not there ; here my makeshift
distinctions would have found things they'd
have been true of . . ."

But that old park, in that old country, exists,
alas and alas, only in Mr. James' mind. . . .

IV

METHODS

THE writing of this little book has proved almost the most thankless—as it is certainly the most formidable—task that I ever undertook. Under protest, as it were, I have written some weary chapters upon our subject's subjects. That, I believe, is demanded in a monograph upon a writer's works and, it would be, I am credibly informed, obtaining attention under false pretences to omit some such speculation. I have written, not so unwillingly, some further chapters—still against the collar—upon Mr. James' temperament, which is the same thing as his "message." I had hoped to do some of the sort of work that I really like doing when I came to the chapter upon this master's methods—upon his "technique."

I can't myself, for the life of me, see that a writer's subjects concern any soul but himself. They have nothing more to do with criticism than eggs with aeroplanes. A critic may like a class of subject or may dislike them—for myself I like books about fox-hunting better than any other book to have a good read in. I would rather read Tilbury Nogo than Daniel Deronda, and any book of Surtees than any book of George Meredith—excepting perhaps Evan Harrington, which is a jolly thing with a good description of country house cricket. But that is merely a statement of preferences, like any other English writing about books. This latter leads the reader, as a rule, no further than to tell him that Messrs. Lang, Collins, or who you will, like reading about golf, Charlotte Corday, the Murder in the Red Barn and, what you will—facts which may be interesting in themselves but which have nothing to do with how a book should be, or is not, written.

Similarly with disquisitions upon the temperament of a writer—since temperament is a thing like sunshine or the growing of grass, a gift of the good God. One may write about it if one likes, if one has nothing better to do ; it is a sort of gossip like any other sort of gossip and, if it does no good in particular, it breaks no bones. Twenty of us, confined in a country house by a south-westerly gale, may well set to work to discuss the temperaments of our friends. " I like so and so," one of us

will say, " he is so considerate " ; " I prefer
Mrs. Dash," another replies, " she is so force-
ful." But all the talk will not make the friend
of So-and-so, with a taste for the milder
virtues, like Mrs. Dash whose attractions are of
a more vigorous type. That is as much as to
say that any penny-a-liner might call your attention to the temperament of Mr. W. H. Hudson,
which is the most beautiful thing that God ever
made, though twenty thousand first-class critics
thundering together could not make Mr. James
like Flaubert. Still, disquisitions upon temperament may do this amount of good :
Supposing that the only work of Mr. James
that you had happened to glance at had been
The Great Good Place, and supposing that you
had no taste for mysticism, preferring the
eerily horrible or the suavely social ! You
would have put Mr. James' volume down and
would have sworn never to take another up.
Then—coming in some newspaper quotation
upon some passage about *The Turn of the
Screw*, which is the most eerie and harrowing
story that was ever written—you might discover that here was a temperament, after all,
infinitely to your taste. So that some profit
might come from that form of writing.

But criticism concerns itself with methods
and with methods and again with methods—

and with nothing else. So that, having waded wearily through a considerable amount of writing that I can only compare to duty-calls, I was rejoicing at the thought of letting. myself go. I felt as a horse does when, after a tiring day between the shafts, it is let loose into a goodly grass field. There seemed to be such reams that one might, all joyfully, write about the methods of this supremely great master of method. I had promised myself the real treat of my life. . . .

But alas, there is nothing to write ! I do not mean to say that nothing could have been written—but it has all been done. Mr. James has done it himself. In the matchless—and certainly bewildering series of Prefaces to the collected edition, there is no single story that has not been annotated, critically written about and (again critically) sucked as dry as any orange. There is nothing left for the poor critic but the merest of quotations.

I desired to say that the supreme discovery in the literary art of our day is that of Impressionism, that the supreme function of Impressionism is selection, and that Mr. James has carried the power of selection so far that he can create an impression with nothing at all. And, indeed, that had been what for many years I have been desiring to say about our master! He can convey an impression, an atmosphere of what you will with literally nothing. Embarrassment, chastened happiness—for his happiness is always tinged with regret—greed, horror, social vacuity—he can give you it all with a purely blank page. His characters will talk about rain, about the opera, about the moral aspects of the selling of Old Masters to the New Republic, and those conversations will convey to your mind that the quiet talkers are living in an atmosphere of horror, of bankruptcy, of passion hopeless as the Dies Iræ! That is the supreme trick of art to-day, since that is how we really talk about the musical glasses whilst our lives crumble to pieces around us. Shakespeare did that once or twice—as when Desdemona gossips about her mother's maid called Barbara whilst she is under the very shadow of death; but there is hardly any other novelist that has done it. Our subject does it, however, all the time, and that is one reason for the impression that his books give us of vibrating reality. I think the word " vibrating " exactly expresses it; the sensation is due to the fact that the mind passes, as it does in real life, perpetually backwards and forwards between the apparent aspect of things and the essentials of life. If you have ever, I mean, been ruined, it will have been a succession of pictures like the following. Things have been going to the devil with you for some time ; you have been worried and worn and badgered and beaten. The thing will be at its climax to-morrow. You cannot stand the strain in town and you ask your best friend—who won't be a friend any more to-morrow, human nature being what it is !—to take a day off at golf with you. In the afternoon, whilst the Courts or the Stock Exchange or some woman up in town are sending you to the devil, you play a foursome, with two other friends. The sky is blue ; you joke about the hardness of the greens ; your partner makes an extraordinary stroke at the ninth hole ; you put in some gossip about a woman in a green jersey who is playing at the fourteenth. From what one of the other men replies you become aware that all those three men know that to-morrow there will be an end of you ; the sense of that immense catastrophe broods all over the green and sunlit landscape. You take your mashie and make the approach shot of your life whilst you are joking about the other fellow's neck-tie, and he says that if you play like that on the second of next month you will certainly take the club medal, though he knows, and you know, and they all know you know, that by the second of next month not a soul there will talk to you or play with you. So you finish the match three up and you walk into the club house and pick up an illustrated paper. . . .

That, you know, is what life really is—a series of such meaningless episodes beneath the shadow of doom—or of impending bliss, if you prefer it. And that is what Henry James gives you—an immense body of work all dominated with that vibration—with that balancing of the mind between the great outlines and the petty details. And, at times, as I have said, he does this so consummately that all mention of the major motive is left out altogether. But it is superfluous for me to say this because it is already said—in a Preface. Consider this :—

Only make the reader's general vision of evil intense enough, I said to myself—

Mr. James is considering how to make *The Turn of the Screw* sufficiently horrible—

—and that already is a charming job—and his own experience, his own imagination, his own sympathy (with the children) and horror (of their false friends) will supply him quite sufficiently with all the particulars. Make him *think* the evil, make him think it for himself, and you are released from

weak specifications. This ingenuity I took pains—
as indeed great pains were required—to apply ; and
with a success apparently beyond my liveliest hope.
. . . How can I feel my calculation to have failed
. . . on my being assailed, as has befallen me, with
the charge of a monstrous emphasis, the charge of
indecently expatiating [upon the corruption of soul
of two haunted children] ? There is . . . not an
inch of expatiation . . . my values are positively all
blanks save so far as an excited horror . . . pro-
ceeds to read into them more or less fantastic
figures. . . .

Here again is one passage which exactly
gives you the measure of how the horror is
suggested. You are dealing with a little boy
who has been expelled from school on a vague
charge. This little boy and his sister have
been corrupted—in ways that are never shown
—by a governess and a groom in whose society
they had been once left and who now, being
dead, haunt, as *revenants*, the doomed children.
The new governess is asking him why he was
expelled from school, and the little boy answers
that he did not open letters, did not steal.

" What then did you do ? "
He looked in vague pain all round the top of the
room and drew his breath two or three times as if
with difficulty. He might have been standing at the
bottom of the sea and raising his eyes to some green
twilight. " Well—I said things."

" Only that ? "

" They thought it enough ! " . . .

" But to whom did you say them ? . . . Was it to every one ? " I asked.

" No, it was only to——" But he gave a sick little headshake. " I don't remember their names."

" Were they then so many ? "

" No—only a few. Those I liked."

" . . . And did they repeat what you said," I went on after a pause. . . .

" Oh, yes," he nevertheless replied—" they must have repeated them. To those *they* liked."

" And those things came round—— ? "

" To the masters ? Oh yes ! " he answered very simply.

I have stripped this episode of all its descriptive passages save one in order to reduce it to the barest and most crude of bones, in order to show just exactly what the hard skeleton is. And it will be observed that the whole matter —the whole skeleton or the only bone of it —is the one word " things " — " I said things."

But, as I have said, Mr. James, unfortunately for me, has uttered already practically all that there is to be said about his own methods. Let us therefore—under the heading of " form "—follow, by means of quotations, his methods in the construction of some of his stories.

HENRY JAMES

Here we have our author, at a dinner, gathering the scheme for a single-figure story[1] :—

For by what else in the world but by fatal design had I been placed at dinner one autumn evening of old London days face to face with a gentleman, met for the first time, though favourably known to me by name and fame, in whom I recognised the most unbridled colloquial romancer the " joy of life " had ever found occasion to envy ? Under what other conceivable coercion had I been invited to reckon, through the evening, with the type, with the character, with the countenance of this magnificent master's wife, who, veracious, serene, and charming, yet not once meeting straight the eyes of one of us, did her duty by each, and by her husband most of all, without so much as, in the vulgar phrase, turning a hair ? It was long ago, but I have never, to this hour, forgotten the evening itself—embalmed for me now in an old-time sweetness beyond any aspect of my reproduction. I made but a fifth person, the other couple our host and hostess ; between whom and one of the company, while we listened to the woven wonders of a summer holiday, the exploits of a salamander, among Mediterranean isles, were exchanged, dimly and discreetly, ever so guardedly, but all expressively, imperceptible lingering looks. It was exquisite, it *could* but become, inevitably, some " short story " or other, which it clearly prefitted as the hand the glove.

[1] Collected Edition.   Preface to Vol. XII.

METHODS

Here again is Mr. James catching hold, at
first hand, of the germ—once more at a dinner-
table—once more with the mind quickly at
work—of *The Spoils of Poynton* [1] :—

So it was, at any rate, that when my amiable
friend, on the Christmas Eve, before the table that
glowed safe and fair through the brown London night,
spoke of such an odd matter as that a good lady in
the north, always well looked on, was at daggers
drawn with her only son, ever hitherto exemplary,
over the ownership of the valuable furniture of a
fine old house just accruing to the young man by his
father's death, I instantly became aware, with my
" sense for the subject," of the prick of inoculation ;
the *whole* of the virus, as I have called it, being infused
by that single touch. There had been but ten words,
yet I had recognised in them, as in a flash, all the
possibilities of the little drama of my *Spoils*,
which glimmered then and there into life ; so that
when in the next breath I began to hear of action
taken, on the beautiful ground, by our engaged
adversaries, tipped each, from that instant, with the
light of the highest distinction, I saw clumsy Life
again at her stupid work. For the action taken, and
on which my friend, as I knew she would, had already
begun all complacently and benightedly further to
report, I had absolutely, and could have, no scrap of
use. . . .

Or here you have Mr. James catching hold
of an idea and, in the very motion of catching

[1] Collected Edition. Vol. X, Preface, p. l.

that golden ball, rendering it more complex and more symmetrical[1] :—

I recognise again, for the first of these three Tales, another instance of the growth of the " great oak " from the little acorn ; since *What Maisie Knew* is at least a tree that spreads beyond any provision its small germ might on a first handling have appeared likely to make for it. The accidental mention had been made to me of the manner in which the situation of some luckless child of a divorced couple was affected, under my informant's eyes, by the re-marriage of one of its parents—I forget which ; so that, thanks to the limited desire for its company expressed by the step-parent, the law of its little life, its being entertained in rotation by its father and its mother, wouldn't easily prevail. Whereas all of these persons had at first vindictively desired to keep it from the other, so at present the re-married relative sought now rather to be rid of it—that is to leave it as much as possible, and beyond the appointed times and seasons, on the hands of the adversary ; which malpractice, resented by the latter as bad faith, would of course be repaid and avenged by an equal treachery. The wretched infant was thus to find itself practically disowned, rebounding from racquet to racquet like a tennis ball or a shuttlecock. This figure could but touch the fancy to the quick and strike one as the beginning of a story—a story commanding a great choice of developments. I recollect, however, promptly thinking that for a proper sym-

[1] Collected Edition.   Vol. XI, Preface.

metry the second parent should marry too—which
in the case named to me indeed would probably soon
occur, and was in any case what the ideal of the
situation required.

And with that we enter at once upon the
vexed and controversial ground of the " handling " that an author may permit himself of
his subject, once he has picked it up.   The
French school of the seventies and eighties—
Maupassant, Flaubert, the Goncourts and the
rest, up to M. France himself—held that a
subject from the life was the merest suggestion.
Once the suggestion was taken hold of, it
should be turned over and over in the mind
until the last drop of suggestion that could
come from the original idea was squeezed out
of it.   So that, in such a masterpiece of this
type as Madame Bovary, or for the matter of
that, Germinie Lacerteux, every incident, every
word, every apparent digression, made towards
the inevitable end.   In that way a feeling of
destiny was produced, a grim semblance of an
implacable outside Providence.   Of course the
real fineness of the art lay in concealing the
art—in making the digressions appear like
real negligences, as they appear in the life we
lead.   Outside this school there has been arising
another, which, for convenience, we may call
the neo-Russian school ;   though, as regards

the construction of their stories, these might almost as well be called neo-Primitives.

The Russians, in fact, like any other peasant people, have an inborn gift of telling stories ; they have no need to be hurried, since for thousands and untold thousands of years they have been peasants without any hope of becoming anything else. They tell, round their stoves, stories of an incredible length for which, since they are also a very patient people, they find ready and attentive listeners. They leave nothing out, they sacrifice nothing in the desire to come more quickly to an end. They go on and on—talking, talking. Their gift is, in fact, the exact inverse of that of the American "anecdotist" or of the Japanese poets who will get an epic into four lines :—

"I went to fetch water from the spring :
I found that a convolvulus had twined its tendrils round
the well-rope.
I went and borrowed water from my neighbour. . . ."

A Russian peasant would take two days in telling that story, giving you the genealogy and the history of the province, the fact that it was necessary to bribe the Governor with rouble notes hidden in bread-offerings, and hour-long dissertations on the goodness of God and the nature of the feelings that it is probable a clinging tendril might have. And this is not merely a matter of selection. It is the self-protective spirit of the race which does not and cannot feel itself safe unless every loophole for objection is closed up. It needs documented reality and documented reality and again documented reality.

In that way you have such writers as the late Count Tolstoy and the late Fyodor Dostoieffsky, story-tellers of the most intense literal realism, with an unrivalled gift for rendering the scenes that they choose for rendering. They choose those scenes, however, without much consideration of whether they have any effect in carrying the story forward, or are of any other use than that of expressing passionate convictions of the author. Between the French schools and the Russian there stands the figure of Turgenieff who had instinctively a great deal of the Frenchman's art—his very first short story is as finished in form as the most perfect of Maupassant's *contes*—and who had a self-effacement unknown otherwise amongst the Russians who are mostly peda-gogues. And the most valuable of all the innumerable matters in Mr. James' Prefaces concerns itself with the beautiful genius as **a** builder up of stories[1] :—

---

[1] Collected Edition. Preface, Vol. III.

I have always fondly remembered a remark that I heard fall years ago from the lips of Ivan Turgenieff in regard to his own experience of the usual origin of the fictive picture. It began for him almost always with the vision of some person or persons, who hovered before him, soliciting him, as the active or passive figure, interesting him and appealing to him just as they were and by what they were. He saw them, in that fashion, as *disponibles*, saw them subject to the chances, the complications of existence, and saw them vividly, but then had to find for them the right relations, those that would most bring them out ; to imagine, to invent and select and piece together the situations most useful and favourable to the sense of the creatures themselves, the complications they would be most likely to produce and to feel.

"To arrive at these things is to arrive at my 'story,' " he said, " and that's the way I look for it. The result is that I'm often accused of not having 'story' enough. I seem to myself to have as much as I need—to show my people, to exhibit their relations with each other ; for that is all my measure. If I watch them long enough I see them come together, I see them *placed*, I see them engaged in this or that act and in this or that difficulty. How they look and move and speak and behave, always in the setting I have found for them, is my account of them—of which I dare say, alas, *que cela manque souvent d'architecture.* But I would rather, I think, have too little architecture than too much—when there's danger of its interfering with my measure of the truth. The French of course like more of it than I give—having by their own genius such a hand for it ; and indeed one must give all one can. As for the origin of one's wind-blown germs themselves, who shall say, as you ask, where *they* come from ? We have to go too far back, too far behind, to say. Isn't it all we can say that they come from every quarter of heaven, that they are *there* at almost any turn of the road ? They accumulate, and we are always picking them over, selecting among them. They are the breath of life—by which I mean that life, in its own way, breathes them upon us. They are so, in a manner prescribed and imposed—floated into our minds by the current of life. That reduces to imbecility the vain critic's quarrel, so often, with one's subject, when he hasn't the wit to accept it. Will he point out then which other it should properly have been ?— his office being, essentially, *to* point out. *Il en serait bien embarrassé.* Ah, when he points out what I've done or failed to do with it, that's another matter : there he's on his ground. I give him up my 'architecture,' " my distinguished friend concluded, " as much as he will."

Mr. James, if he professes himself infinitely grateful to Turgenieff for the service of these hints, nevertheless inclines actually rather to the French method of building up a subject. In a note upon *Daisy Miller*, his earliest " story," he characteristically justifies his proceedings which characterise his later years even more than his former [1] :—

[1] Collected Edition. Vol. XVIII, Preface.

HENRY JAMES

It was in Italy again—in Venice and in the prized society of an interesting friend, now dead, with whom I happened to wait, on the Grand Canal, at the animated water-steps of one of the hotels. The considerable little terrace there was so disposed as to make a salient stage for certain demonstrations on the part of two young girls, children *they*, if ever, of Nature and of freedom, whose use of those resources, in the general public eye, and under our own as we sat in the gondola, drew from the lips of a second companion, sociably afloat with us, the remark that there before us, with no sign absent, were a couple of attesting Daisy Millers. Then it was that, in my charming hostess's prompt protest, the whirligig, as I have called it, at once betrayed itself. " How can you liken *those* creatures to a figure of which the only fault is touchingly to have transmuted so sorry a type and to have, by a poetic artifice, not only led our judgment of it astray, but made *any* judgment quite impossible ? " With which this gentle lady and admirable critic turned on the author himself. " You *know* you quite falsified, by the turn you gave it, the thing you had begun with having in mind, the thing you had had, to satiety, the chance of ' observing ' : your pretty perversion of it, or your unprincipled mystification of our sense of it, does it really too much honour—in spite of which, none the less, as anything charming or touching always to that extent justifies itself, we after a fashion forgive and understand you. But why *waste* your romance ? There are cases, too many, in which you've done it again ; in which, provoked by a spirit of observation

166

at first no doubt sufficiently sincere, and with the measured and felt truth fairly twitching your sleeve, you have yielded to your incurable prejudice in favour of grace—to whatever it is in you that makes so inordinately for form and prettiness and pathos ; not to say sometimes for misplaced drolling. Is it that you've after all too much imagination ? Those awful young women capering at the hotel door, *they* are the real little Daisy Millers that were ; whereas yours in the tale is such a one, more's the pity, as—for pitch of the ingenuous, for quality of the artless—couldn't possibly have been at all." My answer to all which bristled of course with more professions than I can or need report here ; the chief of them inevitably to the effect that my supposedly typical little figure was of course pure poetry, and had never been anything else ; since this is what helpful imagination, in however slight a dose, ever directly makes for.

Thus according to our subject's conscious canons an author is justified in sacrificing, if not the inherent probabilities of his " affair," then at least the photographic realities, to his sense of beauty. Beauty he elsewhere defines as the fun, the interest, the amusingness, the awakening qualities of a story. . . .

Action, that is to say, in the sense of any-body's doing anything, is singularly rare in any of Mr. James' *nouvelles ;* but what the French call *progression d'effet* is never absent from the almost apparently negligible of them.

167

HENRY JAMES

The aspect of the " affair " in hand will change incredibly whilst the characters do no more than sit in arm-chairs or open bookcases. In that sense " *nouvelles* " by this author, however much they may resemble " studies," are never anything of the sort. The treatment of mental progressions is so rare in Anglo-Saxon —and for the matter of that in Latin—fiction that the unsuspecting reader might well mistake the mood of *The Lesson of the Master* for the mood of Bielshin Prairie, which is a true sketch. Mr. James, however, has never, as far as I can recall, given us a real sketch, any more than *Daisy Miller*, which he labels " a study " is a real study. *The Point of View* might pass for one of these, but as a matter of fact it is a true short story, the account of conflicting irresolutions ending in a determination. To a school of readers whose chief pabula are spotless detectives conflicting with besmirched criminals, traffickers in white slaves with unspotted victims, or idle rich with spotless poor and the black generally with the white ; whose " action " is limited to the deciphering of cryptograms, the unveiling of adventuresses, the dismantling of the stage with revolver shots and so on—to the readers of such enlivening fictions the actions and progressions of our author—those conflicts of irreso-

168

lution with irresolution whose only pistol shot
is the arriving at a determination—may well
bear the aspects of studies in metaphysics.
But, actually upon its larger scale and with
its reversing of the order of the incidents, every
short story of Mr. James' is a true short story
—as dependent for surprise upon its last word
as is La Parure. If you will take *The Turn of
the Screw*, with its apparent digressions, its
speculations, its turns and its twists, you will
see that the real interest centres round the
proposition : Is the narrator right or wrong
in thinking that if the little boy can only
disburden himself of a full confession he will
be saved for ever from the evil ascendancy of
Peter Quint. And this hangs in the balance
until the very last sentence settles it :

" We were alone with the quiet day, and his
little heart, dispossessed, had stopped."

Maupassant would have told the story in ten
pages, Mr. James taking one hundred and
fifty. But, though the French genius would
have removed from it the aspect of being a
nouvelle, he could have made it no more of a
conte, except for the shortness. Mr. James'
sense of form is, in fact, so nice as to be unrivalled ; his sense of his subject is nearly as
fierce as Flaubert's ; his digressions are no
more digressions ; his disquisitions no more

disquisitions. If he seldom goes so far as to give us a final sentence like : " *Personne ne croyait que l'Abbé s'était donné la mort,*" he does it—as if to show us that he can— superbly in the sentence I have just quoted. Generally it strikes him as a device too barbaric and one to be shrunk from.

Mr. James, in fact, shrinks from most definite things. Heaven knows there is no reason why he should not shrink from them just as his and our nations—just as all Anglo-Saxondom shrinks from the definite statement. His glass—the poor dear English language and the poor dear Puritan temperament—isn't very big, but it is capable of infinite arabesques. The Latin and the Papist spirit isn't in the least afraid of definition or of coarseness if the defining of a situation calls for coarseness, cynicism or brutality. " Tu es Petrus, et super . . ." we are accustomed to say, taking the words on their face value. . . . But the American and the Englishman, the essential Protestants, shrink from a direct proposition whether it be made by Our Lord or by any other person. And, if they shrink from the hearing of a direct proposition, refining and refining away the incidence, until it appears no more than allegory in the end, still more will they shrink from putting a direct statement into direct words. As I have pointed out elsewhere, when a French peasant sees a suspicious character upon the road, he says : " *C'est qu'que maoufatan* "—" It's some evildoer," the English farm labourer would say : " I guess he's up to no good." And, just as the Anglo-Saxon shrinks from a direct statement of fact—insisting that it shall be said to him instead of " The majority of the House of Commons closured the Budget through "— " *Le Roy remercy ses bons sujets et ainsi le veult*," which is a silly sort of lie—or just as he prefers the allegorical statement : " We handed him a lemon and he quit," to a harsh account of business proceedings, so invariably, wishing all statements made to him—if they are to carry conviction—to be wrapped up in allegory, he is the best Anglo-Saxon who most wraps up his statements.

Mr. James expresses matchlessly his race and its religion. These call for delicate and sympathetic deeds and gentle surmises rather than for clear actions and definite beliefs. So Mr. James first refines all action out of his work —all non-psychological action—and, little by little, sets himself to express himself purely in allegory.

What he has got from abroad is the technique of Form, and in that he has reunited the stream of Anglo-Saxon imagination with the broad stream of international culture. He has in short written, in English, books that are worthy to be read by readers of the great Continental writers. As far as his phraseology goes (and *le style c'est l'homme*) he has expressed his race. And for a man to have attained to international rank with phrases intimately national, is the supreme achievement of writers —a glory that is reserved only for the Dantes, the Goethes and the Shakespeares, who none the less remain supremely national.

I am not saying that the tendency to write allegorically may not be carried too far. To say that " X had not succeeded in planting in his temperate garden a specimen of the rank exotic each of whose leaves is a rustling cheque," may have its disadvantages as well as its advantages considered as a way of expressing the fact that X wrote books that did not pay. It is not at any rate journalese, that flail of the Anglo-Saxon race, that infinite corrupter of the Anglo-Saxon mind, that destined and ultimate cause of the downfall of Anglo-Saxon empires, since the race that cannot either in allegories or in direct speech think clearly is doomed to fall before nations who can; and Japan is ever on the threshold with the tendrils twining round its well-ropes. . . .

METHODS

But the question of the taste for allegorical modes of expression is after all only a question of taste. Personally I should say that Mr. James' " style " strikes me as almost unapproachable up to the day when he concluded *The Spoils of Poynton ;* it is lucid, picturesque and as forcible as it can be, considering that he writes in English. With *What Maisie Knew* it begins to become, as we should say in talking of pheasants, a little " high." And so it goes on until, with the Prefaces and with *A Small Boy*, it just simply soars. There is not any other word for it. . . .

But that is only a question again of taste, and it is very possible that generations trained in the appreciation of this author will find vapid what to me seems clear, and that such a sentence as—the succession of fifty thousand sentences such as : " There at any rate—*for* the story, that is, for the pearl of my idea—I had to take, in the name of the particular instance, no less deep and straight a dive into the deep sea of a certain general truth than I had taken in quest of Flickerbridge."

It obviously means something—they all obviously mean something, the five hundred thousand sentences of the Prefaces, of *A Small Boy*, of *The American Scene*. If you will read them aloud you will find them reasonably

clear. For the latest James—the James of the
latest stage is simply colloquial. Nothing
more and nothing less. It is a matter of
inflexions of the voice much more than of
commas or even of italics. And I have found
repeatedly that when I read a passage aloud,
whether from the Prefaces or *The Golden Bowl*,
it became, to myself at least, infinitely clear,
though no less infinitely embroidered and
decorative.

Whether that implies that, in his latest
phase, Mr. James has been riding his Muse
and his Method to death, or whether it means
that he is sapiently aiming a shaft at oblivion,
I am scarcely concerned to say. It has at
any rate been anticipated that all the novels
of the indefinitely distant future shall be read
out from gramophones to public assemblies.
In *that* Utopia *A Small Boy* would be limpid.

But of this I am certain : Looking upon the
immense range of the books written by this
author, upon the immensity of the scrupulous
labours, upon the fineness of the mind, the
nobility of the character, the highness of the
hope, the greatness of the quest, the felicity
of the genius and the truth that is at once
beauty and more than beauty—of this I am
certain, that such immortality as mankind has
to bestow (most of them haven't any souls !)

METHODS

whether of the talking hooter, or of the silent
pages, will rest upon the author of *Daisy
Miller*. It will rest also with the author of *The
Golden Bowl*.

APPENDIX

APPENDIX

THE following comparisons of passages from the earlier editions of Mr. James', with the same passages revised and amplified for the Definitive Edition, published by Messrs. Macmillan, may be of interest to the reader.

Daisy Miller (Edition: Macmillan, 1883).

" OH, blazes; it's har-r-d ! " he exclaimed, pronouncing the adjective in a peculiar manner.

Winterbourne had immediately perceived that he might have the honour of claiming him as a fellow-countryman. "Take care you don't hurt your teeth," he said, paternally.

" I haven't got any teeth to hurt. They have all come out. I have only got seven teeth. My mother counted them last night, and one came out right afterwards. She said she'd slap me if any more came out. I can't help it. It's this old Europe. It's the climate that makes them come out. In America they didn't come out. It's these hotels."

Winterbourne was much amused. " If you eat three lumps of sugar your mother will certainly slap you," he said.

" She's got to give me some candy, then," rejoined his young interlocutor. " I can't get any candy here

—any American candy. American candy's the best candy."

"And are American little boys the best little boys?" asked Winterbourne.

"I don't know. I'm an American boy," said the child.

"I see you are one of the best!" laughed Winterbourne.

"Are you an American man?" pursued this vivacious infant. And then, on Winterbourne's affirmative reply, "American men are the best," he declared.

His companion thanked him for the compliment; and the child, who had now got astride of his alpenstock, stood looking about him, while he attacked a second lump of sugar. Winterbourne wondered if he himself had been like this in his infancy, for he had been brought to Europe at about this age.

"Here comes my sister!" cried the child in a moment; "she's an American girl."

Winterbourne looked along the path and saw a beautiful young lady advancing. "American girls are the best girls," he said, cheerfully, to his young companion.

"My sister ain't the best!" the child declared. "She's always blowing at me."

"I imagine that is your fault, not hers," said Winterbourne. The young lady meanwhile had drawn near. She was dressed in white muslin, with a hundred frills and flounces, and knots of pale-coloured ribbon. She was bareheaded; but she balanced in her hand a large parasol, with a deep border of embroidery; and she was strikingly, admirably pretty. "How pretty they are!" thought Winterbourne, straightening himself in his seat, as if he were prepared to rise.

The young lady paused in front of his bench, near the parapet of the garden, which overlooked the lake. The little boy had now converted his alpenstock into a vaulting-pole, by the aid of which he was springing about in the gravel, and kicking it up not a little.

"Randolph," said the young lady, "what *are* you doing?"

"I'm going up the Alps," replied Randolph. "This is the way!" And he gave another little jump, scattering the pebbles about Winterbourne's ears.

"That's the way they come down," said Winterbourne.

"He's an American man!" cried Randolph, in his little hard voice.

The young lady gave no heed to this announcement, but looked straight at her brother. "Well, I guess you had better be quiet," she simply observed.

It seemed to Winterbourne that he had been in a manner presented. He got up and stepped slowly towards the young girl, throwing away his cigarette. "This little boy and I have made acquaintance," he said, with great civility. In Geneva, as he had been perfectly aware, a young man was not at liberty to speak to a young unmarried lady except under certain rarely-occurring conditions; but here at Vevey, what conditions could be better than these?—a pretty American girl coming and standing in front of you in a garden. This pretty American girl, however, on hearing Winterbourne's observation, simply glanced at him ; she then turned her head and looked over the parapet, at the lake and the opposite mountains. He wondered whether he had gone too far ; but he decided that he must advance further, rather than retreat. While he was thinking of something else to say, the young lady turned to the little boy again.

Daisy Miller (Definitive Edition, Vol. XVIII., Macmillan, 1909).

" Oh, blazes ; it's har-r-d ! " he exclaimed, divesting vowel and consonants, pertinently enough, of any taint of softness.

Winterbourne had immediately gathered that he might have the honour of claiming him as a country-man. " Take care you don't hurt your teeth," he said paternally.

" I haven't got any teeth to hurt. They've all come out. I've only got seven teeth. Mother counted them last night, and one came out right afterwards. She said she'd slap me if any more came out. I can't help it. It's this old Europe. It's the climate that makes them come out. In America they didn't come out. It's these hotels."

Winterbourne was much amused. " If you eat three lumps of sugar your mother will certainly slap you," he ventured.

" She's got to give me some candy, then," rejoined his young interlocutor. " I can't get any candy here —any American candy. American candy's the best candy."

" And are American little boys the best little boys ? " Winterbourne asked.

" I don't know. *I'm* an American boy," said the child.

" I see you're one of the best ! " the young man laughed.

" Are you an American man ? " pursued this vivacious infant. And then on his friend's affirmative reply, " American men are the best," he declared with assurance.

His companion thanked him for the compliment, and the child, who had now got astride of his alpenstock, stood looking about him while he attacked another lump of sugar. Winterbourne wondered if he himself had been like this in his infancy, for he had been brought to Europe at about the same age.

" Here comes my sister ! " cried his young compatriot. " She's an American girl, you bet ! "

Winterbourne looked along the path and saw a beautiful young lady advancing. " American girls are the best girls," he thereupon cheerfully remarked to his visitor.

" My sister ain't the best ! " the child promptly returned. " She's always blowing at me."

" I imagine that's your fault, not hers," said Winterbourne. The young lady meanwhile had drawn near. She was dressed in white muslin, with a hundred frills and flounces and knots of pale-coloured ribbon. Bareheaded, she balanced in her hand a large parasol with a deep border of embroidery; and she was strikingly, admirably pretty. " How pretty they are ! " thought our friend, who straightened himself in his seat as if he were ready to rise.

The young lady paused in front of his bench,

near the parapet of the garden, which overlooked the lake. The small boy had now converted his alpenstock into a vaulting-pole, by the aid of which he was springing about in the gravel and kicking it up not a little. "Why, Randolph," she freely began, "what *are* you doing ?"

"I'm going up the Alps!" cried Randolph. "This is the way!" and he gave another extravagant jump, scattering the pebbles about Winterbourne's ears.

"That's the way they come down," said Winterbourne.

"He's an American man!" proclaimed Randolph in his harsh little voice.

The young lady gave no heed to this circumstance, but looked straight at her brother. "Well, I guess you'd better be quiet," she simply observed.

It seemed to Winterbourne that he had been in a manner presented. He got up and stepped slowly toward the charming creature, throwing away his cigarette. "This little boy and I have made acquaintance," he said, with great civility. In Geneva, as he had been perfectly aware, a young man wasn't at liberty to speak to a young unmarried lady save under certain rarely-occurring conditions; but here at Vevey what conditions could be better than these ?—a pretty American girl coming to stand in front of you in a garden with all the confidence in life. This pretty American girl, whatever that might prove, on hearing Winterbourne's observation, simply glanced at him; she then turned her head and looked over the parapet, at the lake and the opposite mountains. He wondered whether he had gone too far, but decided that he must gallantly advance rather than retreat. While he was thinking of something else to say the young lady turned again to the little boy, whom she addressed quite as if they were alone together. " I should like to know where you got that pole."

Four Meetings (Edition : Macmillan, 1883).

I saw her only four times, but I remember them vividly ; she made an impression upon me. I thought her very pretty and very interesting—a charming specimen of a type. I am very sorry to hear of her death ; and yet, when I think of it, why should I be sorry ? The last time I saw her she was certainly not—— But I will describe all our meetings in order.

I

The first one took place in the country, at a little tea-party, one snowy night. It must have been some seventeen years ago. My friend Latouche, going to spend Christmas with his mother, had persuaded me to go with him, and the good lady had given in our honour the entertainment of which I speak. To me it was really entertaining ; I had never been in the depths of New England at that season. It had been snowing all day, and the drifts were knee-high. I wondered how the ladies had made their way to the house ; but I perceived that at Grimwinter a conversazione offering the attraction of two gentlemen from New York was felt to be worth an effort.

Mrs. Latouche, in the course of the evening, asked me if I " didn't want to " show the photographs to some of the young ladies. The photographs were in a couple of great portfolios, and had been brought home by her son, who, like myself, was lately returned from Europe. I looked round, and was struck with the fact that most of the young ladies were provided with an object of interest more absorbing than the most vivid sun-picture. But there was a person standing alone near the mantel-shelf, and looking round the room with a small gentle smile which seemed at odds, somehow, with her isolation. I looked at her a moment, and then said, " I should like to show them to that young lady."

" Oh, yes," said Mrs. Latouche, " she is just the person. She doesn't care for flirting ; I will speak to her."

I rejoined that if she did not care for flirting, she was, perhaps, not just the person ; but Mrs. Latouche had already gone to propose the photographs to her.

" She's delighted," she said, coming back. " She is just the person, so quiet and so bright." And then she told me the young lady was, by name, Miss Caroline Spencer, and with this she introduced me.

Four Meetings (Definitive Edition, Vol. XVI, Macmillan, 1909).

I SAW her but four times, though I remember them vividly ; she made her impression on me. I thought her very pretty and very interesting—a touching specimen of a type with which I had had other and perhaps less charming associations. I'm sorry to hear of her death, and yet when I think of it, why *should* I be ? The last time I saw her she was certainly not——! But it will be of interest to take our meetings in order.

I

The first was in the country, at a small tea-party, one snowy night of some seventeen years ago. My friend Latouche, going to spend Christmas with his mother, had insisted on my company, and the good lady had given in our honour the entertainment of which I speak. To me it was really full of savour— it had all the right marks : I had never been in the depths of New England at that season. It had been snowing all day and the drifts were knee-high. I wondered how the ladies had made their way to the house ; but I inferred that just those general rigours rendered any assembly offering the attraction of two gentlemen from New York worth a desperate effort.

Mrs. Latouche in the course of the evening asked me if I " didn't want to " show the photographs to some of the young ladies. The photographs were in a couple of great portfolios, and had been brought home by her son, who, like myself, was lately returned from Europe. I looked round and was struck with the fact that most of the young ladies were provided with an object of interest more absorbing than the most vivid sun-picture. But there was a person alone near the mantel-shelf who looked round the room with a small vague smile, a discreet, a disguised yearning,

which seemed somehow at odds with her isolation.
I looked at her a moment and then chose. "I
should like to show them to that young lady."

"Oh, yes," said Mrs. Latouche, "she's just the
person. She doesn't care for flirting—I'll speak to
her." I replied that if she didn't care for flirting she
wasn't perhaps just the person; but Mrs. Latouche
had already, with a few steps, appealed to her par-
ticipation. "She's delighted," my hostess came back
to report; "and she's just the person—so quiet and
so bright." And she told me the young lady was by
name Miss Caroline Spencer—with which she introduced me.

Four Meetings (Edition : Macmillan, 1883).

I RESENTED extremely this scornful treatment of poor
Caroline Spencer's humble hospitality; but I said
nothing, in order to say nothing uncivil. I only looked
on Mr. Mixter, who had clasped his arms round his
knees and was watching my companion's demonstra-
tive graces in solemn fascination. She presently saw
that I was observing him; she glanced at me with a
little bold explanatory smile. "You know, he
adores me," she murmured, putting her nose into
her tapestry again. I expressed the promptest
credence, and she went on. "He dreams of becoming
my lover ! Yes, it's his dream. He has read a French
novel; it took him six months. But ever since

that he has thought himself the hero, and me the heroine ! "

Mr. Mixter had evidently not an idea that he was being talked about ; he was too preoccupied with the ecstasy of contemplation. At this moment Caroline Spencer came out of the house, bearing a coffee-pot on a little tray. I noticed that on her way from the door to the table she gave me a single quick, vaguely-appealing glance. I wondered what it signified ; I felt that it signified a sort of half-frightened longing to know what, as a man of the world who had been in France, I thought of the Countess. It made me extremely uncomfortable. I could not tell her that the Countess was very possibly the runaway wife of a little hair-dresser. I tried suddenly, on the contrary, to show a high consideration for her. But I got up ; I couldn't stay longer. It vexed me to see Caroline Spencer standing there like a waiting-maid.

" You expect to remain some time at Grim-winter ? " I said to the Countess.

She gave a terrible shrug.

" Who knows ? Perhaps for years. When one is in misery ! . . . *Chère belle*," she added, turning to Miss Spencer, " you have forgotten the cognac ! "

I detained Caroline Spencer as, after looking a moment in silence at the little table, she was turning away to procure this missing delicacy. I silently gave her my hand in farewell. She looked very tired, but there was a strange hint of prospective patience in her severely mild little face. I thought she was rather glad I was going. Mr. Mixter had risen to his feet and was pouring out the Countess's coffee. As I went

back past the Baptist church I reflected that poor
Miss Spencer had been right in her presentiment
that she should still see something of that dear old
Europe.

Four Meetings (Definitive Edition, Vol. XVI,
Macmillan, 1909).

I RESENTED extremely so critical a view of my poor
friend's exertions, but I said nothing at all—the only
way to be sure of my civility. I dropped my eyes on
Mr. Mixter, who, sitting cross-legged and nursing his
knees, watched my companion's foreign graces with an
interest that familiarity had apparantly done little to
restrict. She became aware, naturally, of my mystified
view of him and faced the question with all her boldness.
" He adores me, you know," she murmured with her
nose again in her tapestry—" he dreams of becoming
mon amoreux. Yes, *il me fait une cour acharnée*—
such as you see him. That's what we've come to.
He has read some French novel—it took him six
months. But ever since that he has thought himself
a hero and me—such as I am, monsieur—*je ne sais
quelle dévergondée !* "

Mr. Mixter may have inferred that he was to that
extent the object of our reference ; but of the manner
in which he was handled he must have had small
suspicion—preoccupied as he was, as to my companion, with the ecstasy of contemplation. Our
hostess moreover at this moment came out of the
house, bearing a coffee-pot and three cups on a neat
little tray. I took from her eyes, as she approached
us, a brief but intense appeal—the mute expression,

APPENDIX

as I felt, conveyed in the hardest little look she had
yet addressed me, of her longing to know what, as a
man of the world in general and of the French world in
particular, I thought of these allied forces now so
encamped on the stricken field of her life. I could
only " act " however, as they said at North Verona,
quite impenetrably—only make no answering sign.
I couldn't intimate, much less could I frankly utter,
my inward sense of the Countess's probable past, with
its measure of her virtue, value and accomplishments,
and of the limits of the consideration to which she
could pioperly pretend. I couldn't give my friend a
hint of how I myself personally " saw " her interesting
pensioner—whether as the runaway wife of a too-
jealous hair-dresser or of a too-morose pastry-cook,
say ; whether as a very small bourgeoise, in fine,
who had vitiated her case beyond patching up, or
even as some character, of the nomadic sort, less
edifying still. I couldn't let in, by the jog of a shutter,
as it were, a hard informing ray and then, washing
my hands of the business, turn my back for ever,
I could on the contrary but save the situation, my
own at least, for the moment, by pulling myself
together with a master hand and appearing to ignore
everything but that the dreadful person between us
was a " grande dame." This effort was possible
indeed but as a retreat in good order and with all
the forms of courtesy. If I couldn't speak, still less
could I stay, and I think I must, in spite of everything,
have turned black with disgust to see Caroline Spencer
stand there like a waiting-maid. I therefore won't
answer for the shade of success that may have

191

attended my saying to the Countess, on my feet and as to leave her : " You expect to remain some time in these *parages ?* "

What passed between us, as from face to face, while she looked up at me, *that* at least our companion may have caught, that at least may have sown, for the after-time, some seed of revelation. The Countess repeated her terrible shrug. " Who knows ? I don't see my way— ! It isn't an existence, but when one's in misery— ! *Chère belle,*" she added as an appeal to Miss Spencer, " you've gone and forgotten the ' *fine* ' ! "

I detained that lady as, after considering a moment in silence the small array, she was about to turn off in quest of this article. I held out my hand in silence —I had to go. Her wan set little face, severely mild and with the question of a moment before now quite cold in it, spoke of extreme fatigue, but also of something else strange and conceived—whether a desperate patience still, or at last some other desperation, being more than I can say. What was clearest on the whole was that she was glad I was going. Mr. Mixter had risen to his feet and was pouring out the Countess's coffee. As I went back past the Baptist church I could feel how right my poor friend had been in her conviction at the other, the still intenser, the now historic crisis, that she should still see something of that dear old Europe.